GOING PRO WITH
REASON™ 6.5

G. W. Childs IV

Course Technology PTR
A part of Cengage Learning

COURSE TECHNOLOGY
CENGAGE Learning·

Australia • Brazil • Japan • Korea • Mexico • Singapore • Spain • United Kingdom • United States

COURSE TECHNOLOGY
CENGAGE Learning·

Going Pro with Reason™ 6.5
G. W. Childs IV

Publisher and General Manager,
Course Technology PTR: Stacy L. Hiquet

Associate Director of Marketing:
Sarah Panella

Manager of Editorial Services:
Heather Talbot

Senior Marketing Manager:
Mark Hughes

Acquisitions Editor: Orren Merton

Project and Copy Editor: Marta Justak

Technical Reviewer: Chris Petti

Interior Layout Tech: MPS Limited

Cover Designer: Mike Tanamachi

Indexer and Proofreader: Kelly Talbot

For product information and technology assistance, contact us at
Cengage Learning Customer & Sales Support, 1-800-354-9706

For permission to use material from this text or product, submit all requests online at **cengage.com/permissions**

Further permissions questions can be emailed to
permissionrequest@cengage.com

Reason is a trademark of Propellerhead Software. All other trademarks are the property of their respective owners.

All images © Cengage Learning unless otherwise noted.

Library of Congress Control Number: 2012930799

ISBN-13: 978-1-4354-6008-9

ISBN-10: 1-4354-6008-1

Course Technology, a part of Cengage Learning

20 Channel Center Street

Boston, MA 02210

USA

Cengage Learning is a leading provider of customized learning solutions with office locations around the globe, including Singapore, the United Kingdom, Australia, Mexico, Brazil, and Japan. Locate your local office at:
international.cengage.com/region

Cengage Learning products are represented in Canada by Nelson Education, Ltd.

For your lifelong learning solutions, visit **courseptr.com**

Visit our corporate website at **cengage.com**

Printed in the United States of America
1 2 3 4 5 6 7 13 12

To my family: Bill, Suzanne, Allison, Tommy, Alex, Jennifer, Haley, Lexie, Will, Elizabeth, and Ruby. You all make it so much more fun.

Acknowledgments

Thanks to God for giving me the ability to work on wonderful projects like these, with wonderful people.

Thank you to the Cengage team:

Orren Merton, Heather Talbot, Mark Hughes, and everyone else who helped make this book happen. It's an honor to work with you guys.

Thank you to Marta Justak. Your attention to detail and ability to see things ahead has made this a wonderful book. It wouldn't have been the same without you.

Chris Petti—thank you for coming on board and keeping it real. It was a pleasure to work with you. Your knowledge and skill really helped this book in a big way.

Sincere thanks to Propellerhead, for making a program that has grown into something so amazing and versatile.

Thanks to the third-party developers:

Magnus Lidstrom (Sonic Charge), Kurt Kurasaki (Peff), and Rob Papen. Your products really helped tie this book together. Great work, guys.

Thanks to Garald and Jimmy at Avoca Coffee. It's always nice to have a great little coffee shop to do your work in.

Thanks to Pamela Moncrief for keeping things fun while I'm feverishly writing to get this book completed.

Thanks to Juan, Brad, Austin, Jason H and Jason P, John, Jose, Braiden and the rest of the gang at the Usual. When my head needs a break from Reason, it's good to be able to hang out with you guys.

About the Author

G. W. Childs IV (www.gwchilds.com) is no stranger to Reason. As a sound designer for Reason, G.W. has worked very closely with the developers and third-party developers in helping to make Reason what it is today. In addition to working with Propellerhead, G.W. has also been involved in several video game productions, such as *Star Wars: Battlefront, Star Wars: Knights of the Old Republic: The Sith Wars, The Old Republic, The Force Unleashed, Mercenaries,* and more. These days, he spends his time in Texas, spreading the joy of Reason and frequenting coffee shops.

Contents

Introduction ix

Chapter 1 Setting Up Reason   1

Reason's Setup Wizard 1
Setting Up Your Audio 1
Setting Up Your Sampling Input 3
Setting Up a MIDI Controller 6
    Setting Up a MIDI Controller That Is Not Listed in Reason 7
Using More Than One MIDI Controller with Reason 9
Default Song (or Template) 10
The Scratch Disk Folder 11
Conclusion 12

Chapter 2 Song Creation Workflows in Reason   13

How Does Reason's Sequencer Differ from Other Applications? 14
Important Navigational Keyboard Commands 14
Recording with Virtual Instruments 19
    Creating an Instrument 19
    Setting Up to Record an Instrument 23
    Recording MIDI with a Virtual Instrument 25
MIDI Editing in Reason 29
Conclusion 34

Chapter 3 Arrangement and Composition Tricks   37

Blocks 37
    Using the Blocks Feature as a Marker System 37
    Remixing with Blocks 43
Easily Laying Down Drums for Remixes 53
Conclusion 59

Chapter 4 Deeper into Drums   61

Turning a Weakness into a Strength 61
    Pattern Conversion to MIDI 61
    Splitting Up Drums Parts into Separate MIDI Clips and Tracks 63
Grouping 67
    Setting Up Multiple Audio Outputs for Drums 67

Setting Up and Controlling Insert FX from the Mix Channel 76
    Adding an Insert Effect to a Mix Channel and Programming the Rotaries for Console Access 76
    Creating Easy Fills with Dub Tracks 82
    Sidechaining in Reason for Drums 87
Conclusion 93

Chapter 5 Sampling in Reason
                                                                        95

Sampling Instruments in Reason 95
    Sampling Inputs and Reconfiguration Possibilities 96
    A Note About Dr. Octo Rex 97
Sampling and Editing 97
Velocity Mapping with Kong and Other Samplers 101
    Sample Pitch 105
Using Multiple Hits from NN-Nano for Multi-Mapping 106
Converting Audio to Samples 108
NN-XT: The Sampler Powerhouse of Reason 116
    Tuning and Mapping a Real Instrument in the NN-XT 116
Conclusion 119

Chapter 6 Cords and Combinators
                                                                        121

The Power of the Combinator 122
Subtractor with Matrix in a Combinator 122
Effects Within a Combinator 133
Conclusion 143

Chapter 7 Effects Combinators
                                                                        145

The Combinator for FX 146
Basic Effects Combinator 147
Conclusion 166

Chapter 8 MIDI Controlled Effects
                                                                        167

Neptune 167
    Neptune Major Features 168
    Neptune Control Voltage Features 168
    Neptune as an Insert (Robotic Style) 169
    Setting Up a MIDI Controlled Effect 171
    Neptune for Backing Vocals 174
    Conclusion to Neptune 174
BV512 Vocoder 175
    Major Features 175
    The Back Panel 176
    Setting Up the Classic Vocoder Effect (More Robot) 177

Contents

Alligator 183

    Major Features 183

    Control Voltage and Audio I/O Functionality 184

    Using the Alligator as an Insert with MIDI Control 185

Conclusion 189

Chapter 9 Rack Extensions   191

VST/AU? 192

The Reason Back Panel 192

Getting New Rack Extensions 193

    Installing Rack Extensions 194

    When "Tried" REs Expire 198

    Checking the Expiration Dates on Your REs 201

Rack Extensions: Effects 203

    Polar by Propellerhead 203

    Redrum and Polar Together—An Exercise 205

    Softube Saturation Knob 210

    Bitspeek by Sonic Charge 212

    Buffre by Peff 215

RE Instruments 218

    Korg Polysix 218

Conclusion 222

Index   223

Introduction

Reason is an amazing application that has been built upon solid layers of programming for several versions at this point. If you're just now getting to know Reason, or you're looking to take your skill with Reason to the next level, you couldn't have picked a better time in its long history of excellence. As of Reason 6.5, Propellerhead has now opened the door to third-party developers to add additional instruments and effects to Reason in the form of Rack Extensions. But beyond the inclusion of new blood, over the past couple of versions, Reason truly has become an all-in-one studio that has few rivals.

What You'll Find in This Book

Within these pages, you'll be given the knowledge you need to integrate Reason into your workflow with valuable information that includes:

▷ Eye-opening walk-throughs in using Reason's most powerful instruments and effects.
▷ Detailed information on settings and options that give you insider information on optimizing Reason for your system.
▷ In-depth exercises that will open up your creative mind to the powerful possibilities available to you for taking your music to the next level.

Who This Book Is For

This book is intended for an audience that already has a basic to advanced background with music software and studio recording. It has been written for the user who already has either a studio, or project studio, and would now like to add in Reason as an additional tool.

How This Book Is Organized

This book is organized in a logical order, assuming that you have just picked up the software and have finished installing it. From this point, it takes you on a full walk-through of what's possible with Reason, and highlights options that you may not have ever thought were available. To sum it up, this book is perfect for someone who has been around the block with music software and would just like to get to work.

Chapter Overview:

1. **Chapter 1, "Setting Up Reason":** Get set up in Reason for audio and MIDI, and learn how to tweak the settings in a way that will make Reason comfortable for you every time you sit down to use it.
2. **Chapter 2, "Song Creation Workflows in Reason":** Begin learning valuable key commands, the differences between Reason and other applications, and how to record with Reason's virtual instruments.
3. **Chapter 3, "Arrangement and Composition Tricks":** Learn all you need to know about the innovative Blocks system installed in Reason. You'll be able to get all the parts of your song together quickly and figure out how to arrange with ease. Additionally, you'll begin learning how to work with drums in Reason.

4. **Chapter 4, "Deeper into Drums":** Begin learning valuable techniques for mixing drums, insert effects, and sidechaining. You also will get valuable suggestions for keeping your session organized.

5. **Chapter 5, "Sampling in Reason":** Wrap your head around age-old sampling concepts like key mapping, velocity mapping, recording samples, inputs, and the Reason sample editor. If you're doing Hip Hop, House, Trance, Industrial, or EBM, you need to check this chapter.

6. **Chapter 6, "Cords and Combinators":** Begin jumping into one of the things that really sets Reason apart from all other DAWs—Combinators. You'll also begin working in the back panel of Reason, where all the audio and control voltages are located. This is where the true power of Reason exists!

7. **Chapter 7, "Effects Combinators":** Learn how to create intricate and amazing effects processors of your own through the Combinator. If you're an audio tweaker, this is the chapter for you.

8. **Chapter 8, "MIDI Controlled Effects":** Reason has some effects that can do things to audio, in conjunction with a MIDI controller, that shouldn't even be allowed. Learn amazing devices like Neptune that can help make even the roughest vocal session sound that much better. Learn the Alligator, a device that can make a simple note sound like an ensemble of instruments. There's something for everyone in this chapter.

9. **Chapter 9, "Rack Extensions":** New to Reason 6.5, Rack Extensions finally gives third-party developers the ability to create instruments and effects for Reason. Get a look at some of the awesome new gear that you can purchase, not only to enhance but also to individualize your Reason rack.

Setting Up Reason

I N THIS CHAPTER, we're going to cover the basics of getting Reason up and running so that you can get started quickly. If at any point you feel like you're sufficiently set up for your needs, feel free to move farther in the book.

Reason's Setup Wizard

When you start Reason for the first time, you'll be prompted to answer a few questions so that Reason can configure itself based on your hardware. If you're at the wizard at this moment, I'd suggest canceling, and we'll run through it together, so that I can give you some more elaborate explanation for what the preferences mean, and how they affect you. To cancel the Setup Wizard, simply push the Cancel button (see Figure 1.1).

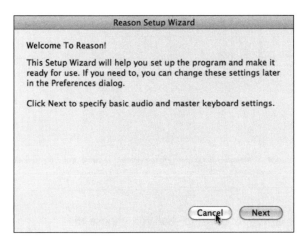

Figure 1.1 Cancel the Setup Wizard.
Source: Propellerhead Software.

Setting Up Your Audio

Before you can do anything, the audio needs to be set up.

1. Go to Reason Preferences (see Figure 1.2). On the Apple, go to the Reason menu → Preferences. On the PC, it's Edit → Preferences.

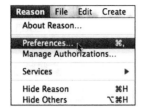

Figure 1.2 Choose Preferences from the Reason menu.
Source: Propellerhead Software.

2. Select the Audio page from the menu at the top, as shown in Figure 1.3.

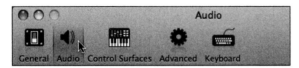

Figure 1.3 Select the Audio page.
Source: Propellerhead Software.

3. Select your audio device from the Audio Device drop-down menu (see Figure 1.4). On the PC, it's important to select the ASIO version of the device that you own.

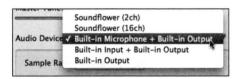

Figure 1.4 Choose an available audio device.
Source: Propellerhead Software.

Built-in Sound?

On the Apple, if you plan on using the built-in sound on your laptop, make sure that you choose the option Built-In Microphone+Built-In Output. Using this feature enables you to record with the Macbook's built-in microphone, which can be cool for jam sessions at coffee shops, impromptu vocal recordings, and so on.

4. Adjust your Buffer Size to around 256, as shown in Figure 1.5.

Figure 1.5 Adjust the Buffer Size of Reason.
Source: Propellerhead Software.

Buffer Size Settings

A buffer size of 256 is good to start with because there's hardly any noticeable latency with instruments and the audio still sounds good. If you're on an uber machine, try lower. If you're on an older machine, and you're having problems, try around 512.

5. If you're using an audio device with multiple inputs/outputs, you'll want to enable the inputs/outputs that you plan on using. Press the Channels button next to the Active Input Channels and enable the inputs you want (see Figure 1.6).

Figure 1.6 The audio inputs section.
Source: Propellerhead Software.

6. Press the Channels button next to the Active Output Channels and enable the Outputs (see Figure 1.7).

Figure 1.7 The audio outputs section.
Source: Propellerhead Software.

This completes a basic audio setup. Now, let's talk about the Sampling Input.

Setting Up Your Sampling Input

Audio inputs 1and 2, by default, are the Sampling Input channels for Reason's sampling devices. Reason's samplers work exactly like the hardware samplers of old, and they actually have Sample buttons that trigger recording instantly. After the recording is complete, the recording is mapped across the keys like a traditional sampler.

The devices with this function are:

▷ Redrum
▷ NN-XT
▷ NN-19
▷ Kong

Default Mapping for Drums

With Redrum and Kong, the samples are mapped to specific keys only, the exact way a drum machine maps. In fact, it's very similar to how General MIDI devices map drums across keyboards, or if you MIDI an old Roland drum machine to a MIDI keyboard. The kick drum will usually be on C1, the snare on D1, the closed hi-hat on F#1 and so on. So, as you're going through the Reason drum patches, you'll notice this trend in mapping repeated. The sound designers were intentional with this, along with Propellerhead, so that when General MIDI drum files are brought in to Reason, the drums will play appropriately.

If you plan on sampling with Reason, and would prefer to use a different set of audio inputs for your audio interface, please follow the instructions below. For example, if your microphone is hooked up to input 7, you'll want to route a cable from input 7 on the back of the Reason Hardware Interface to the Sampling Input channels.

To modify the Sampling Input:

1. Press F6 to go to the rack page, as shown in Figure 1.8. (In Chapter 2, "Song Creations Workflow in Reason," we'll cover more hot keys for navigation.)

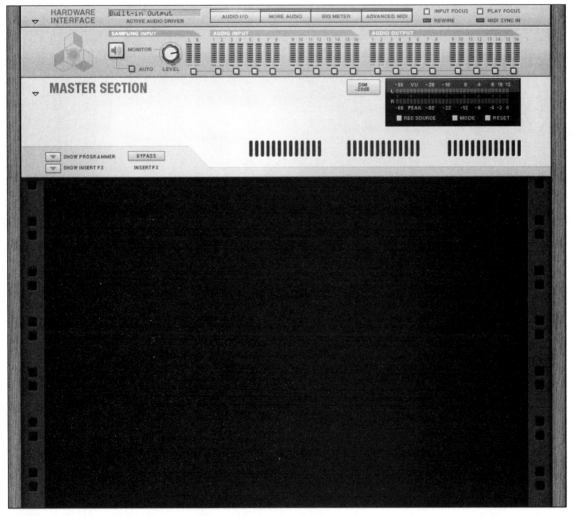

Figure 1.8 Reason Hardware Interface and Master Section.
Source: Propellerhead Software.

2. Press the Tab button to turn the rack around (see Figure 1.9).

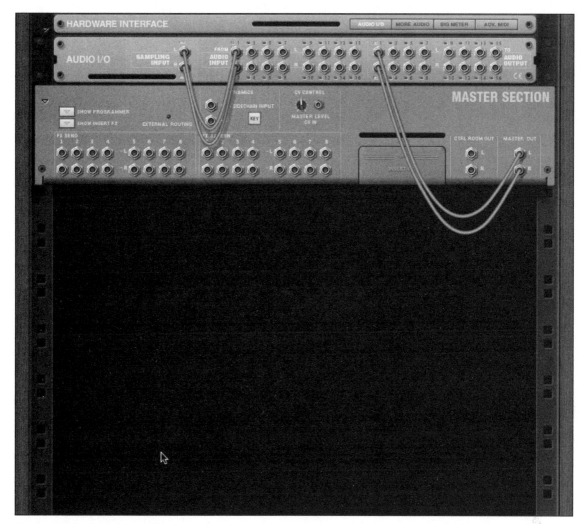

Figure 1.9 The back of the Reason Hardware Interface and Master Section.
Source: Propellerhead Software.

3. Drag the cables from audio inputs 1 and 2, which are going to the Sampling Input, to the inputs that your microphone or audio inputs are connected to (see Figure 1.10).

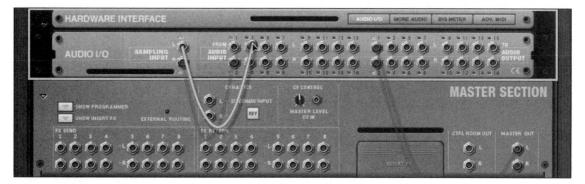

Figure 1.10 Changing the input going into the Sampling Input.
Source: Propellerhead Software.

If you want the Sampling Input to go to the same channels with each new session, you'll need to set up your default template to launch automatically with this input each time. See the section in this chapter on "Default Template."

Setting Up a MIDI Controller

This section walks you through setting up a MIDI controller. It's important to note that several control surfaces, like the Euphonix MC series, rely on Mackie Control, as opposed to using their own drivers when working with Reason. Therefore, it's imperative that you also read the manual on some of the bigger control surfaces before using them with Reason.

If you're just setting up a MIDI keyboard, this should be a piece of cake.

It's important to note before beginning that Reason has a large library of controllers embedded within the program. This is a protocol known as Remote, developed by Propellerhead. If your controller is detected and a picture appears next to it, this will mean that your version of Reason fully supports the controller, as it has Remote mappings created specifically for Reason This also means that all of its functions are mapped to the knobs available, regardless of which Reason instrument or device you select and plan on controlling. Regardless of whether you have a Remote mapped controller or not, follow the setup procedures below.

1. In the Preferences pane, go to the Control Surfaces page (see Figure 1.11).

Figure 1.11 Selecting the Control Surfaces page in Reason Preferences.
Source: Propellerhead Software.

2. In the Control Surfaces page, if you have already installed all of the software that came with your MIDI controller device, press the Auto-Detect Surfaces button (see Figure 1.12).

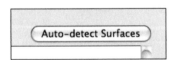

Figure 1.12 The Auto-Detect Surfaces button.
Source: Propellerhead Software.

When Reason Doesn't Find Your Controller

Usually, Reason will find your controller on its own. If it doesn't, it could be that you are using one of the following:

▶ A MIDI keyboard that is connected via a MIDI interface to your computer through actual MIDI ports, as opposed to USB. This would mean it's a generic MIDI controller in Reason's way of looking at things.

▶ Your MIDI controller does not have the Remote software supporting it installed. If this is the case, visit the website of your MIDI controller's manufacturer and see if they actually have Propellerhead's Remote software for your particular controller.

▶ There is no Remote software supporting Reason for your controller.

If any of the above mentioned in the tip is the case, move on to step 3.

3. Once Reason is through looking for your connected devices, it will place a picture next to them and you are ready to go (see Figure 1.13). If no picture is listed, carry on to the next section.

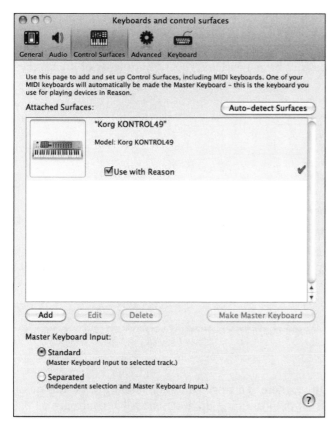

Figure 1.13 A Korg controller supported as a Remote mapped device.
Source: Propellerhead Software.

Setting Up a MIDI Controller That Is Not Listed in Reason

If no Remote driver is available, meaning that there is no picture and your device is not listed within Reason, then you'll need to do a manual setup of your controller. To do this, follow these steps:

1. Press the Add button at the bottom of the Keyboards and Control Surfaces page (see Figure 1.14).

Figure 1.14 The Add button in the Keyboard and Control Surfaces page.
Source: Propellerhead Software.

2. From the window that appears, choose Other from the Manufacturer drop-down menu (see Figure 1.15).

Figure 1.15 Select Other from the Manufacturer drop-down list.
Source: Propellerhead Software.

3. From the Model drop-down menu, choose what type of device you are trying to set up. For example, if you are setting up a control surface, a device that does not have a MIDI keyboard but plenty of knobs, then choose control surface (see Figure 1.16).

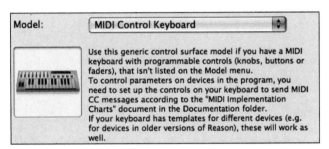

Figure 1.16 A generic MIDI controller shown in the Reason preferences.
Source: Propellerhead Software.

Read About Your Controller!

After you select any of the models listed under Other, there is a small paragraph stating what this model type is intended for. I would urge you to read this if you are setting up a generic MIDI controller.

4. Rename your listed controller to whatever you'd like it to be called within Reason, as I have done in Figure 1.17.

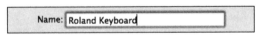

Figure 1.17 Rename the controller name.
Source: Propellerhead Software.

5. Now, you'll need to choose which MIDI port your input device is coming through (see Figure 1.18). The easiest way to do this is to press the Find button and then try to play your keyboard. Reason will look for the MIDI signal and choose the correct port.

Figure 1.18 The Find MIDI Input page as it appears in Reason.
Source: Propellerhead Software.

Once Reason has selected a port, you're ready to go and can close the Preferences menu. Or you can carry on to some of the next setup procedures.

If you need to set up more than one controller, please continue on to the next section.

Using More Than One MIDI Controller with Reason

It is possible to use several MIDI devices with Reason. In fact, it's one of the best applications out there for it, in terms of how much you can map controller functions to certain Reason instrument and effect devices.

If you need to set up more than one MIDI controller, follow the steps below, as you'll want to be in Separated mode.

1. Set up additional devices the way you did in the previous section.
2. Locate the Master Keyboard Input at the bottom of the Controllers page (see Figure 1.19).

Figure 1.19 The Master Keyboard Input section.
Source: Propellerhead Software.

3. Because you are using more than one controller, specifically more than one MIDI keyboard, select Separated. When in Separated mode, you have the ability to deselect MIDI control on a track by simply deselecting the keyboard that appears on each Reason track when selected.

> ## Rewire and MIDI
>
> If you are going to be using Reason as a Rewire slave, with Pro Tools, Logic Pro, Ableton, and so on, then you should use Separated mode. This will save you a lot of hassle when you switch back to the host DAW to use one of the non-Reason instruments.

Default Song (or Template)

You may reach a point where you want Reason to launch or start a new song with a particular set of devices.

In most applications, this is known as a *default template*. In Reason, this feature is known as *Default Song*. Let's go through how to set this up.

1. Go to Reason Preferences, as shown in Figure 1.20.

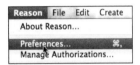

Figure 1.20 Select Reason Preferences.
Source: Propellerhead Software.

2. Go to the General page in Preferences (see Figure 1.21).

Figure 1.21 Select the General page in Reason Preferences.
Source: Propellerhead Software.

3. Locate the Default Song section of the General page (see Figure 1.22).

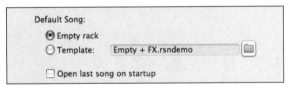

Figure 1.22 The Default Song section of the General page.
Source: Propellerhead Software.

4. As you can see, you have a few options for what kind of song Reason can launch with.

   ▷ **Empty rack:** There are no instruments or devices, period. You are starting from a blank slate. This is my personal favorite.

▷ **Template:** You choose a song file that Reason will start with every time it launches by pushing the blue folder button next to this option.

▷ **Open Last Song on Startup:** Choose this option if you would prefer that Reason start up with the last song you were working on when you closed Reason.

It's important to note that Reason comes with a slew of handy templates that may resemble exactly what you're looking for. After pressing the blue folder button, choose the Reason Folder (see Figure 1.23) and then choose the Templates folder.

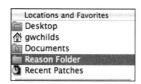

Figure 1.23 The Reason Folder as it appears in the Reason Browser.
Source: Propellerhead Software.

See if there's a description listed that matches what you're after, or you can browse to a song file of your own that has all of your favorite devices loaded with your favorite patches.

Create Your Own Startup Song!

Making your own start-up song is easy. Simply create a song file in Reason that has all of your favorite devices. These devices can even be loaded with instrument patches that you use a lot, effects patches, and so on. Once you have the whole layout exactly the way you want to see it, save the song in a location on your hard drive where you know it won't be disturbed. Then, in Reason Preferences → General Page, browse with the blue folder button, next to the Template option under Default Song, to the song file you created and select it. Voilà, Reason will start up with this song every time.

5. Select whichever option suits you best. Or check off Open Last Song on Startup.

The Scratch Disk Folder

The Scratch Disk is where Reason holds all of your recording data for new songs—those being songs that you are working on and haven't saved yet. It's important to be aware of this if you're working off a laptop with limited space on its hard drive.

Low on Space?

If you are on a hard drive with limited space, I'd strongly encourage you to invest in an external, portable hard drive that you can carry around with you. There's nothing worse than getting a "You are out of space" message when you're in the middle of a recording session.

If you need to change the Scratch Disk location, follow these steps:

1. Go to Reason Preferences.
2. Go to the Advanced page, as shown in Figure 1.24.

Figure 1.24 Select the Advanced page.
Source: Propellerhead Software.

3. Locate the Scratch Disk Folder section of the Advanced page (see Figure 1.25).

Figure 1.25 The Scratch Disk Folder section of the Advanced page.
Source: Propellerhead Software.

4. Press the Change button. This will open a browser that prompts you to choose a new folder on either your internal or external hard drive.

The Scratch Disk

The Scratch Disk can always be moved to another location by simply pressing the Reset button. If the scratch disk is not present when Reason boots up, this will happen anyway.

Conclusion

Okay, this takes care of the basic setup of Reason. As you can see, there's not much to it. In the next chapter, we're going to look at some of the major hot keys and key commands that you really need to know for Reason, as well as tricks and tips for recording and editing that will make your life much easier. We'll also be covering the major windows of Reason and what they do. Reason is an extremely versatile piece of software that doesn't require you to know everything about it to get the job done, but it does help to know what the major sections of the software are.

Song Creation Workflows in Reason

I N THE PAST, Reason was in many cases used as a sketchpad, where the song would be built and the final product would be produced in another program. Part of its charm in being a brilliant sketchpad was its stability and its portability. Reason has just never relied on outboard gear.

Also, I tend to credit Reason's sequencer. It's really streamlined, and doesn't inundate you with features. Everything is laid out simply and precisely. If you want advanced features, those are carefully hidden away in the Tools menu, which we'll discuss later in this chapter.

In the most recent version of Reason, the sequencer has gotten even more formidable with the Blocks function. This feature essentially is a clever form of pattern sequencing, where you can create multiple loops, known as *Blocks*, and then later, chain each Block in any particular order to form the makeup of your song.

In this chapter, we'll be focusing on the sequencer, and I'll guide you through familiar workflows in software platforms, only within the framework of Reason.

Keep in mind, we'll be covering some basic things in this chapter that you may not feel you need. If it looks like you've got all this information already, move on to the next chapter. But, know this, I am covering several keyboard commands that make getting around in Reason much simpler. I would at least encourage a glance through this chapter if you're a key command junky.

How Does Reason's Sequencer Differ from Other Applications?

If you've worked in Logic Pro, Pro Tools, Cubase, or even Garageband, you'll actually find Reason's sequencer and songwriting workflows to be very similar. Where Reason has been designed to emulate classic hardware and signal flow, the sequencer has also been designed as a clever amalgamation of many different sequencers. One of the biggest differences between Reason and other software sequencers out there would be the fact that, unlike other major applications, it is tightly integrated with not only the virtual instruments, but is also designed to work with Reason's unique, pattern-based devices, effects, and even its amazing pro mixer. Because the devices are native to Reason and aren't VST, AU, DX, and so on, the sequencer capabilities, in terms of automation, are seamless. When you mix this with features like Blocks, Regroove, and thoughtful touches like Alt and Dub tracks, you get a very formidable sequencer.

But I'd also like to point out something that others may not tell you. Many of the other DAWs have pumped their sequencers with so many different features that they have often overcomplicated what is supposed to be a very simple process—making music! The designers at Propellerhead seem to have really gone to great lengths to keep Reason's sequencer very streamlined. Don't get me wrong, the features are all there, but they have made accessing the features extremely intuitive. In the end, this means that someone who's had a lot, or even a little, experience with other applications will pick up Reason easily. And, if you're one of the rare producers who still relies more on hardware than computers, but has decided to give virtual devices a chance, you'll be in heaven. No other application out there emulates hardware as well as Reason.

Important Navigational Keyboard Commands

Before we move too far into the inner workings of the sequencer, I'd like to bring a few keys on your QWERTY keyboard to your attention that are essential for navigating Reason. These buttons will let you move through the three windows of Reason easily, rather than having to drag around different pages. Instead, with a press of a button, a page is presented which is exactly what you are looking for. I've also included some of the smaller windows that play a major part in using Reason.

To access the sequencer:

Press the F7 button.

Pressing this button on your keyboard brings up the sequencer page (see Figure 2.1), no matter where you are currently located within Reason.

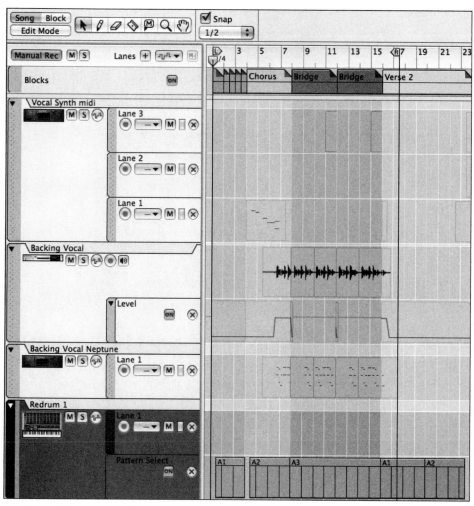

Figure 2.1 The Reason sequencer.
Source: Propellerhead Software.

To access the rack:

Press the F6 button.

Pressing this button brings up the Reason hardware rack (as shown in Figure 2.2), where all of your virtual instruments and effects exist and can be modified.

Figure 2.2 The Reason rack.
Source: Propellerhead Software.

To access the mixer:

Press the F5 button.

Pressing this button brings up the mixer page within Reason (as shown in Figure 2.3), which is used to mix, engineer, and produce your final song.

Figure 2.3 The Reason mixer.
Source: Propellerhead Software.

To access the Tool window:

Press the F8 button.

This button brings up the Tool window (as shown in Figure 2.4), which contains the advanced sequencer, editing features, a "draggable" instrument palette that contains all the devices within Reason, Groove Settings, and the Song Samples page, which contains a very handy audio editor for editing samples.

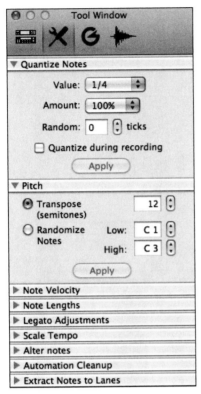

Figure 2.4 The Reason Tool window.
Source: Propellerhead Software.

To access the On-screen Piano Keys:

Press the F4 button.

This may seem like a trivial, novice feature. Do not be fooled! This is a very handy window (see Figure 2.5) that enables you to use your typing keyboard as a music keyboard, and it is particularly great if you don't have a MIDI controller. If you are touring or flying a lot, keep this one in mind. It has two pages: one page for triggering keyboard keys with a mouse and one page for the keyboard.

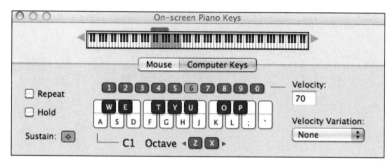

Figure 2.5 On-screen Piano Keys.
Source: Propellerhead Software.

Recording with Virtual Instruments

Now that we have the major key commands of Reason out of the way, let's do some actual recording. The most common method of recording in Reason uses its well-renowned virtual instruments, so let's do that first and then we'll go on to audio recording.

Let's create an instrument that we can use to record.

Creating an Instrument

Reason has a large selection of instruments and effects, but these devices are seemingly prepared as very specific devices that only exist within a virtual domain. What if you want a piano, or rock drums, or something else?

Reason does offer a very clever solution for instruments in the form of the Create Instrument function. When this command is triggered, you are able to search the All Instruments folder in the Reason Factory Sound Bank, which is broken down into subdirectories with labels like Pianos, Drums, and so on.

This is especially handy when you're working with an act that has specifically asked for a certain instrument. Using the Create Instrument function, you can quickly find 20 pianos.

It is also possible to have Reason search for specific instrument types for you, using the Reason Patch Browser.

1. In an empty Reason session, hold down the Command (Ctrl) button and press the letter I. This will bring up the Reason Patch Browser, as shown in Figure 2.6.

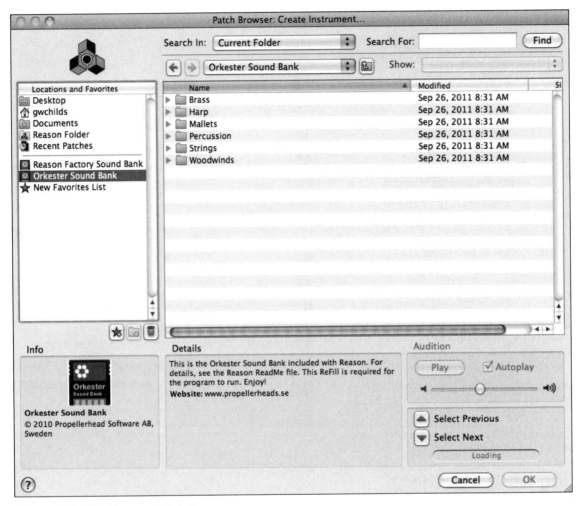

Figure 2.6 The Reason Patch Browser.
Source: Propellerhead Software.

2. Select the Reason Factory Sound Bank in the left-hand side of the Reason Patch Browser (see Figure 2.7).

Figure 2.7 The Reason Factory Sound Bank listed in the Reason Patch Browser.
Source: Propellerhead Software.

3. Type in Piano in the upper right-hand corner of the Reason Patch Browser. You may also choose any other instrument you prefer, such as Guitar, Bass, Drums, or you can be even more specific, like Fat Bass, House Kit, and so on (see Figure 2.8).

Figure 2.8 Use the Reason Patch Browser to find a specific instrument type.
Source: Propellerhead Software.

4. Press the Find button or press the Return or Enter button (see Figure 2.9).

Figure 2.9 Press the Find button to discover a specific instrument type.
Source: Propellerhead Software.

5. The middle section of the Reason Patch Browser will now show several different pianos (see Figure 2.10). Note that if you have a MIDI controller connected, you can simply highlight a piano in the list and start playing to demo how the piano sounds. Keep highlighting pianos and playing until you find a sound you like.

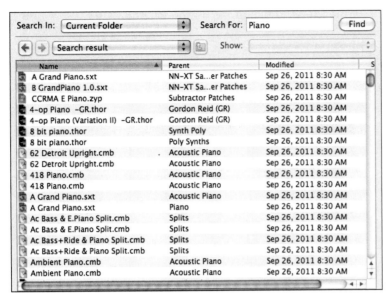

Figure 2.10 The Reason Patch Browser, listing all of the different pianos after a search.
Source: Propellerhead Software.

6. When you have found an instrument or patch that you would like to work with, press the OK button at the bottom (see Figure 2.11).

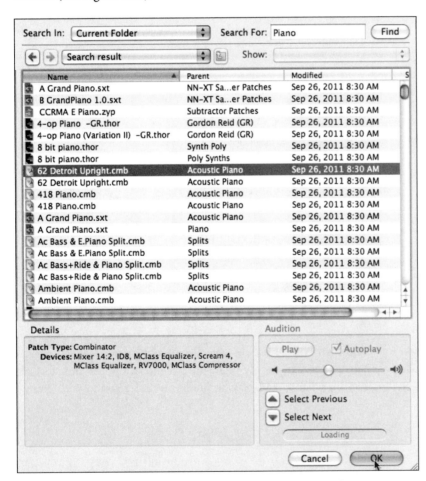

Figure 2.11 Confirm a piano choice in the Reason Patch Browser.
Source: Propellerhead Software.

7. After pressing OK, your selected instrument will appear in the Reason rack page. This device will at the same time be represented in the Mixer page and the Sequencer page (see Figure 2.12). You'll notice that in the sequencer lane within the Sequencer page, there is a small instrument icon (not shown), indicative of the instrument providing the sound you are using.

Figure 2.12 The selected piano instrument as it appears in the Reason rack as a Combinator.
Source: Propellerhead Software.

Now that you have the instrument created and your sound dialed in, let's take a look at a few options to consider enabling.

Setting Up to Record an Instrument

There are a few features that I would suggest enabling and setting up before recording. These options are the following:

▷ **Q Rec (Auto Quantize):** This option automatically quantizes anything you record, without the annoying procedure of going back and highlighting a clip, pressing Quantize, and so on (see Figure 2.13). The default quantize resolution is 16th notes. This default can be changed in the Tool window → Sequencer Tools → Quantize Notes, which really speeds up your workflow and the overall tightness of the song.

Figure 2.13 Select Q Rec or Auto Quantize.
Source: Propellerhead Software.

▷ **Loop mode:** This option is similar to the Loop mode in Cubase or the Cycle mode in Logic (see Figure 2.14). When enabled, the sequencer loops between two points in the arrangement section of the sequencer. In Reason, these points are the L and R locators.

Figure 2.14 Select Loop mode on the Reason transport bar.
Source: Propellerhead Software.

You can drag the loop locators to your desired location, or you can hold down the Option (Ctrl) button and click in the time timeline to move the Left loop locator instantly. To move to the (R) Right loop locator, you can drag or hold down Command (Alt) and then click in the timeline (see Figure 2.15).

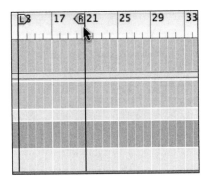

Figure 2.15 The loop locators as they appear in the sequencer.
Source: Propellerhead Software.

You can also type in the desired location of each loop locator and then press the Return key (Enter) directly underneath the Loop button on the transport bar. The L and R buttons denote the positions for each locator. Press the corresponding L and R buttons to instantly position the Song Position pointer (playback needle) at the desired loop locator (see Figure 2.16).

Figure 2.16 Use the Reason transport to send a loop locator to a specific destination.
Source: Propellerhead Software.

▷ **Click track (or Metronome):** Of course, we all need a click track when recording, unless you have perfect timing. Right! Press the Click button to enable the Metronome or click track within Reason (see Figure 2.17). The volume of the click can be adjusted independently of the overall Reason volume with the Click Level knob next to it.

Figure 2.17 Enable the Metronome or Click button in Reason.
Source: Propellerhead Software.

▷ **Pre (Count-in):** If you don't want the click going through the whole song while you are recording, but want a way to Count-in before the recording starts, enable the Pre button (see Figure 2.18). If the click is on, you still get a Count-in as well. The volume of the Pre, or Count-in, is also controlled by the Click Level knob.

Figure 2.18 Enable the Pre or Count-in.
Source: Propellerhead Software.

▷ **Tempo and Tap Tempo**: You can adjust the overall tempo of your beginning track with the Tempo (see Figure 2.19).You can simply use the Up and Down arrows next to the displayed Tempo. Or you can type in the desired tempo and press Return or Enter. You can also press the Tap button repeatedly along with someone playing, or you can use the beat of a song that you want the tempo of a given track to emulate. As you tap, the Tempo will adjust automatically.

Figure 2.19 Press the Tap Tempo.
Source: Propellerhead Software.

▷ **Time Signature**: Time signature is adjusted directly to the right of the Tempo indicator on the transport bar of Reason. Simply click and type in the signature that you like.

You now have an idea of the recording options available in Reason. Not all of these are necessary with the beginning of every new song or recording; however, I do find the Q Rec, Loop markers, and Click and Pre options very handy, and would encourage their use so that you can keep your recordings tight.

Let's move on to recording a virtual instrument in Reason.

Recording MIDI with a Virtual Instrument

If you've followed along up to this point, you're ready to begin recording. If not, take a look at the last couple of exercises that show you how to set up an instrument, as well as set up options that will assist you in creating tight recordings.

In this exercise, we're simply going to record an instrument part, using the instrument created in the earlier "Creating an Instrument" exercise. The options enabled from the "Setting Up to Record an Instrument" exercise are purely up to you; however, the Q Rec, Click, and Pre are mandatory for this exercise. If you aren't sure what these are, refer to the previous section for more help.

1. Begin a Reason session that contains just a virtual instrument and nothing else (see Figure 2.20). We'll get to other instruments later. I'll be using a piano for this exercise.

Figure 2.20 The rack with a Combinator instrument.
Source: Propellerhead Software.

2. Go to the Sequencer page by pressing F7. Notice that your instrument is sitting snugly within a lane, waiting for you to play and record it (see Figure 2.21).

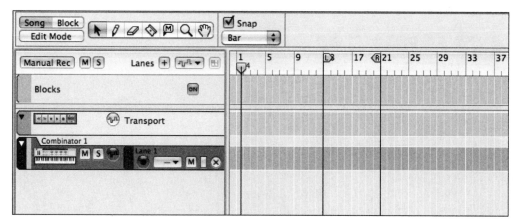

Figure 2.21 A virtual instrument as it appears in the sequencer.
Source: Propellerhead Software.

3. (Optional) Position your loop locators for recording with the loop record (see Figure 2.22). Option+Click (Ctrl+Click) in the timeline to move the left loop marker. Press Cmd+Click (Alt+Click) in the timeline to move the Right loop locator. When these are set up to your liking, enable the Loop button on the transport bar (not shown).

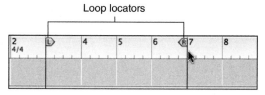

Figure 2.22 Position the loop locators.
Source: Propellerhead Software.

4. Enable your Click button to keep yourself in time (see Figure 2.23).

Figure 2.23 Enable the click feature to stay in time with Reason.
Source: Propellerhead Software.

5. Enable Q Rec (see Figure 2.24).

Figure 2.24 Enable Auto Quantize, or Q Rec.
Source: Propellerhead Software.

6. Position the Song Position pointer where you want to start recording (see Figure 2.25). If you're using the loop locators, I'd suggest positioning the song pointer on the Left loop locator for a tight loop. To move the Song Position pointer, simply click in the timeline.

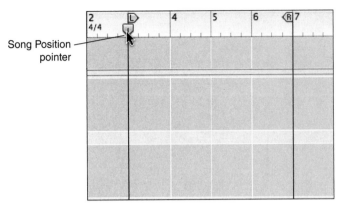

Figure 2.25 Position the Song Position pointer.
Source: Propellerhead Software.

7. Press the Record button to begin recording (see Figure 2.26). You may also press the Enter button on the keypad controller on a full keyboard, or you can press Cmd+Return (or Ctrl+Enter) to start recording.

Figure 2.26 Press the Record button on Reason's transport.
Source: Propellerhead Software.

8. If you are in Loop Record mode, you can just keep adding notes as the loop repeats (see Figure 2.27). This can be especially handy when recording drums. When you are finished recording, press the spacebar on your computer keyboard.

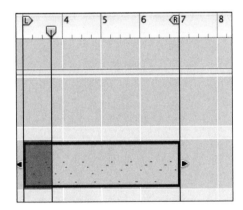

Figure 2.27 Loop recording in the Reason sequencer.
Source: Propellerhead Software.

You've now finished your first recording. No doubt you'd probably like to fix any mistakes you've made at this point. This would be the perfect time to take a look at MIDI editing in Reason.

MIDI Editing in Reason

It's inevitable that you'll run into a situation where your MIDI recording take is almost perfect, but if you could just tweak that one note, everything would be exactly the way you hear it in your head.

In this exercise, let's take a look at moving, deleting, and modifying notes in the MIDI editor. Reason's edit functions are very simple, but quite powerful. Pay close attention to the key commands presented within this exercise, because you'll be using them again in other exercises moving forward.

You'll notice that when you finished recording, a small rectangular "clip" was left in the sequencer representing your recording. This is where the MIDI data is stored. Let's go inside this clip, as it's called in Reason.

1. Either double-click on the MIDI clip you created in the last exercise when recording or you can press Cmd+E on your keyboard (Ctrl+E). There is also an Edit Mode button that you can push in the sequencer to enter this area of the Reason sequencer (see Figure 2.28). Finally, you can highlight a specific clip and press the Return button. This will put you into Edit mode as well.

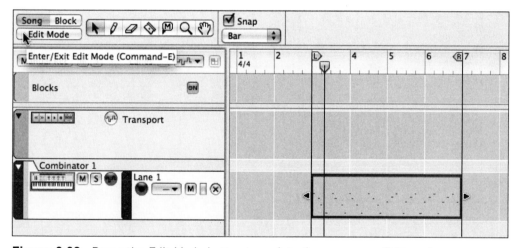

Figure 2.28 Press the Edit Mode button to go into the sequencer Edit mode.
Source: Propellerhead Software.

2. Now you're in Edit mode. In this mode, you'll see all the small squares that represent the notes that you played in the last exercise. If you tap on any of the notes, you'll hear the piano, or whatever instrument you chose, sound off proudly. Try this now, as I have done in Figure 2.29.

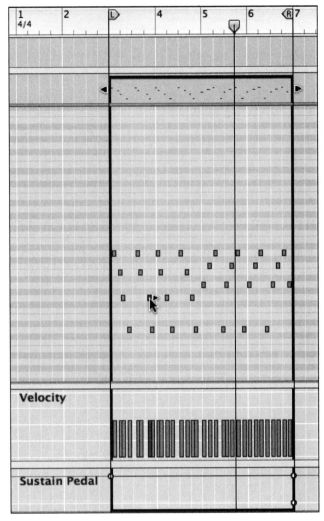

Figure 2.29 Select two notes in the sequencer Edit mode.
Source: Propellerhead Software.

Disabling Sound

If you would prefer that the note did not sound off when tapped, go to Reason Preferences and disable the Trigger Notes While Editing function. This feature can be actually annoying if you are someone who edits while the notes are playing looped in the sequencer.

3. Notice that when you tapped the note, it became darker and a small arrow appeared next to it. Additionally, you'll find that position data, length data, note information, and velocity levels appear at the top (see Figure 2.30). What's cool about this is that you can manually type in the position where you'd like the note to be located and how long you'd like it to continue. You can even change the note to the exact note you'd like it to be. Try changing the note now by typing in the note and then pressing the Return or Enter button.

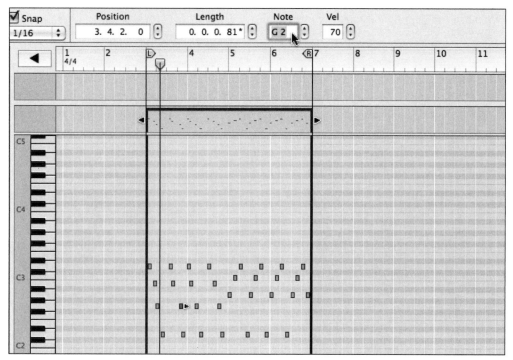

Figure 2.30 Change a programmed note to a different key by typing.
Source: Propellerhead Software.

4. If you prefer to manually drag notes around, that's OK. You can move notes around by dragging them in the sequencer as well. Try this now, as shown in Figure 2.31.

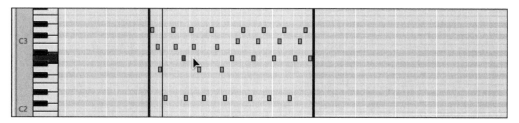

Figure 2.31 Drag notes around in the Reason sequencer.
Source: Propellerhead Software.

5. You can also change the length of the note with the small arrow that appears directly to the left of each note. If you hover over the note arrow, you'll notice that your cursor icon changes to arrows (see Figure 2.32). When this indicator appears, try clicking and dragging left or right. Notice how the note gets longer or shorter.

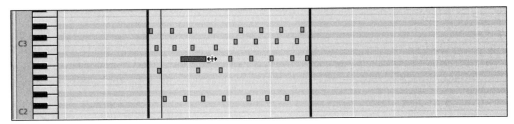

Figure 2.32 Increase the length of a note.
Source: Propellerhead Software.

6. If you need to copy a note, here's an easy trick. Click on the note and hold it. While holding, press the Option button (or Alt). While holding both buttons, drag the note to the location that you would like the copy to appear. As you do this, you'll notice the original note stays and the new copy is now being moved, as shown in Figure 2.33.

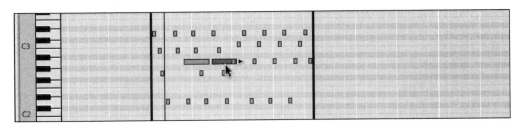

Figure 2.33 Copy a note.
Source: Propellerhead Software.

Copy Multiple Notes

You may prefer to copy multiple notes. To do this, drag-select a box around all the notes you want, so that they all darken. Next, hold down Cmd (Ctrl) and tap C. Move the Song Position pointer to where you want the notes to start and hold down Cmd (Ctrl) and press V, as shown in Figure 2.34.

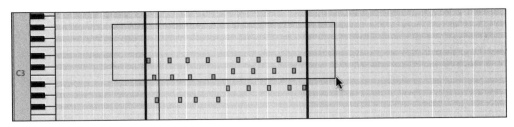

Figure 2.34 Drag-select multiple notes.
Source: Propellerhead Software.

7. You may want to copy in a note that plays faster than what is currently a 16th note resolution. If you want to draw in a 32nd, 64th, or 128th note resolution, adjust the snap up at the top (see Figure 2.35). It is also possible to copy with the snap setting so that multiple notes will play in quick succession. This is incredibly helpful when editing hi-hats, drum rolls, stutter effects, arpeggiations, and so on.

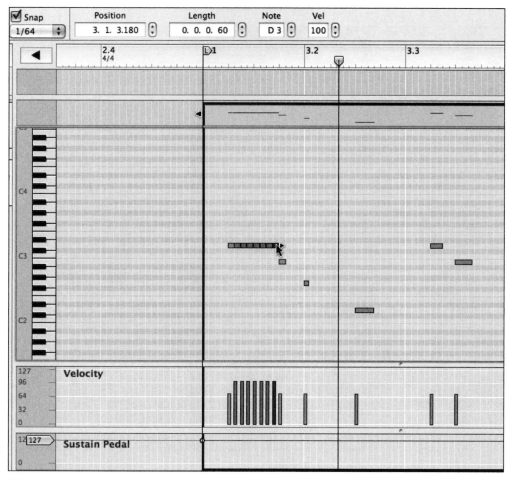

Figure 2.35 Copy multiple notes after adjusting the snap value.
Source: Propellerhead Software.

How to Draw in Notes

To draw new notes, you can either select the Pencil tool or hold down the Cmd (Alt) button in the sequencer window, and the cursor will automatically change to a pencil (see Figure 2.36).

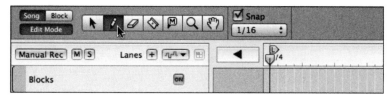

Figure 2.36 Select the pencil tool.
Source: Propellerhead Software.

8. You'll notice that the velocities for each note are at the bottom of Figure 2.37. You can manually increase and decrease the velocities with the Pencil tool, hold down the Cmd (Alt) button, and have the Pencil tool appear at random. If multiple notes are selected and you edit velocities with the pencil while holding the Shift button, only the selected note velocities will be edited.

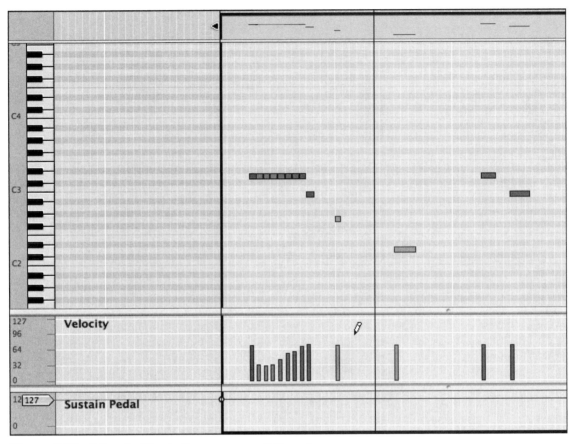

Figure 2.37 Edit velocities in the sequencer Edit mode.
Source: Propellerhead Software.

9. When you are ready to leave Edit mode, press the Edit Mode button or press Cmd+E (Ctrl+E). You can also use the ESC button to leave Edit mode, as well.

Conclusion

At this point, you've probably noticed how familiar Reason's way of working is in comparison to other programs on which you may have worked. There's not a lot of reinventing the wheel going on here. It's straightforward, quick, and simple.

If you're used to certain features in other audio applications, but they aren't appearing so far, don't worry! As we get deeper into Reason, you may find what you are looking for, and even a few things you never had before. You may even try key commands from other applications. For example, I always used the Option+Drag command to copy notes in Cubase. I was very happy to discover this function was also available in Reason when I tried it.

Thus far, we've gotten to know the basics of recording, editing, and setting up for MIDI recording. We've also gotten some very pertinent key commands out of the way that will really help you moving forward. In the next chapter, we'll explore tricks that utilize the Blocks features and much more.

Arrangement and Composition Tricks

I N THIS CHAPTER, we're going to start stepping into some advanced tricks in the sequencer that are complete life changers, once you know about them.

For this chapter, we'll be focusing on the Blocks feature and how it can speed up remixing.

Blocks

The Blocks feature of Reason is an addition that really slid by the wayside for many people. But for those who adopted it as a system of song creation, it became a whole new way of working.

For many, the "never-ending loop," a term that I use all the time, has become a virtual graveyard for many a song. The melody is great, but it never gets past being a three- or four-bar loop. Most professionals have had to get past this frustrating black hole, but even professionals can benefit from new systems, especially when they speed up the writing and arrangement process.

The intention behind the Blocks feature is the implementation of a pattern-based song creation system within Reason. Essentially, you'll copy parts or create parts within a Block. Keep in mind, you aren't just creating Blocks with one instrument at a time, you're actually filling Blocks with several different parts, based on what you have within your Reason rack.

Once you've finished creating all of your different Blocks, you can just draw out the arrangement at the top of the sequencer in Song mode.

This is all well and good, and I'm sure you'll enjoy the traditional uses of Blocks. I'd like to show you one trick, though, that can help in a way you may not have thought of.

Using the Blocks Feature as a Marker System

Reason has been used by many professional artists, producers, and composers for years and years. With this in mind, you'd think that Propellerhead would have implemented a marker system for keeping track of what happens where in your arrangements!

Well, in all actuality, the Blocks system can be used as a very effective marker system in its own right. Think about it! It's up at the top of the sequencer, it can be colored, and it tints the regions below for easy identification.

Let's see how this feature works.

1. In the File menu, select Open (see Figure 3.1).

Figure 3.1 The Reason File menu.
Source: Propellerhead Software.

2. Select the Reason Folder and then, in the Browser area, select Demo Songs. Double-click Olivia Broadfield - Say.rsndemo, as shown in Figure 3.2.

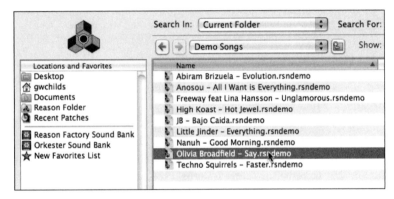

Figure 3.2 Select the Olivia Broadfield demo.
Source: Propellerhead Software.

3. This song is perfect, because there are no Blocks set up for this song at all. Go ahead and enable the Blocks function at the bottom of the screen on the transport bar (see Figure 3.3).

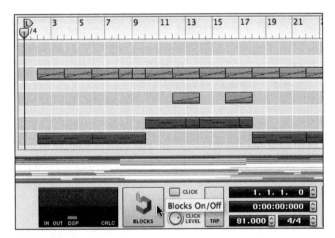

Figure 3.3 Enable Blocks.
Source: Propellerhead Software.

4. Now the Blocks lane appears at the top of the sequencer page (see Figure 3.4).

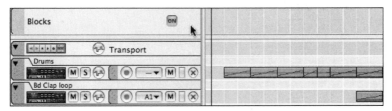

Figure 3.4 The Blocks lane in the sequencer page.
Source: Propellerhead Software.

5. Hold down the Cmd or Alt button, while hovering over the Blocks lane. You'll notice the mouse cursor turns into a pencil (see Figure 3.5).

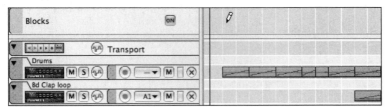

Figure 3.5 The pencil tool in the Blocks lane.
Source: Propellerhead Software.

6. Draw a Block from measures 2–10 (see Figure 3.6). Even though there is nothing going on inside the Block, we're using it to identify the first eight measures of the song, and identify it like a marker system. Notice how a colored region tints the sequence below. This will really help later in identifying what part of the song is what. Even if you can't see the top of the screen, it's still color-coded.

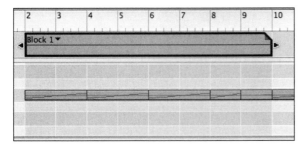

Figure 3.6 Draw a Block for identification purposes.
Source: Propellerhead Software.

7. Press the B button, which will take you into Block mode (see Figure 3.7).

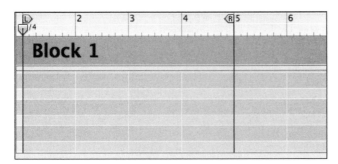

Figure 3.7 The Reason Block mode.
Source: Propellerhead Software.

8. Double-click where it says Block 1, which will allow you to type in this area (see Figure 3.8).

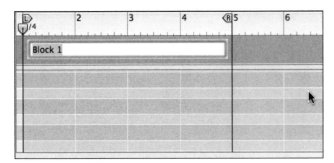

Figure 3.8 Double-click Block 1 to rename it.
Source: Propellerhead Software.

9. Type in Verse 1 and press Return (see Figure 3.9).

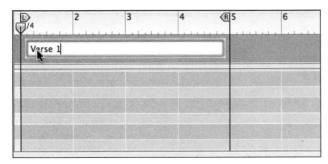

Figure 3.9 Renaming Block 1.
Source: Propellerhead Software.

10. Press the B button to return to the regular Sequencer mode (not shown).
11. Draw in another Block in the Block lane from measures 10–18. Notice, it will be labeled Verse 1, too, as shown in Figure 3.10. Don't worry, we'll fix that.

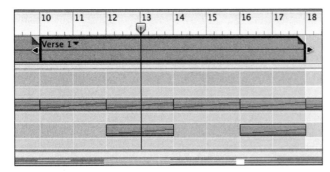

Figure 3.10 Draw in a Block from measure 10–18.
Source: Propellerhead Software.

12. Press the B button again to go to Blocks mode. While inside, select the Blocks drop-down menu and select Block 2 (see Figure 3.11).

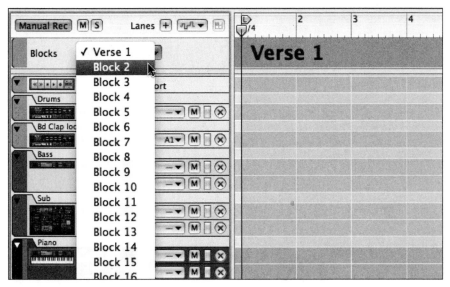

Figure 3.11 The Blocks drop-down menu.
Source: Propellerhead Software.

13. Double-click where it says Block 2 and change it to Chorus 1, as shown in Figure 3.12.

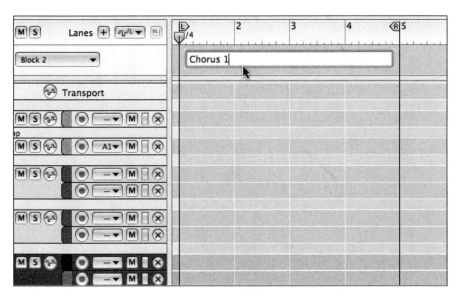

Figure 3.12 Relabel Block 2 to Chorus 1.
Source: Propellerhead Software.

14. Press B again and go back to the Song mode.

15. In the Song mode, on the Block you recently created, click the small arrow where it says Verse 1. This will bring up a drop-down menu. Select Chorus 1, as shown in Figure 3.13.

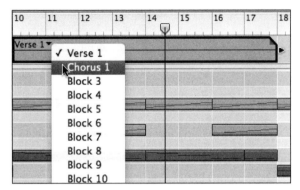

Figure 3.13 Change the Block name in the drop-down menu.
Source: Propellerhead Software.

16. Now, you'll notice that Reason automatically chose a different color from your first Block. If you would like to use a different color for this marker, simply right-click on the second Block and select Color (see Figure 3.14).

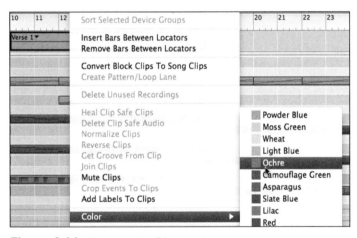

Figure 3.14 Change the Block color.
Source: Propellerhead Software.

Changing colors and differentiating among the major sections of your songs will really help you in keeping track of what's going on in your arrangements. And, as you probably already know, markers are extremely helpful when you're working on a project with someone else, such as remix artists, producers, engineers, and so on. With markers, they can visually see what's going on in your arrangements, rather than clicking around and hoping they don't eliminate something important.

Another cool thing is that once you've finished with your initial arrangement of your song, and you decide you'd like to make a couple of other versions (for example, a remix, a radio edit, an extended version, etc.), you can copy each section of your arrangement, handily indicated by your markers, into each of the corresponding Blocks to make new arrangements easily. We will try this out.

Remixing with Blocks

In this exercise, we'll continue with the beautiful demo from Olivia Broadfield, using the edits that we made in the last exercise. That being the case, this exercise assumes that you already set up the Blocks as prescribed by the last exercise.

1. Set your Snap to 1/2 notes, as shown in Figure 3.15.

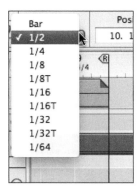

Figure 3.15 Adjust your Snap resolution.
Source: Propellerhead Software.

2. Tighten up the Verse 1 Block where it starts at Measure 1.3 and ends at Measure 9.3 (see Figure 3.16). You may need to zoom in to really get this tight.

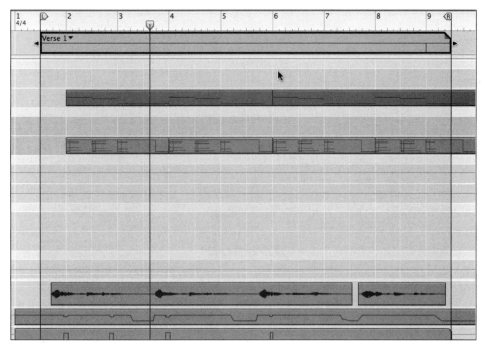

Figure 3.16 Tighten up the Verse 1 Block.
Source: Propellerhead Software.

3. Modify the Chorus 1 Block so that it's actually starting at 9.3 and ending at 17.3, as shown in Figure 3.17.

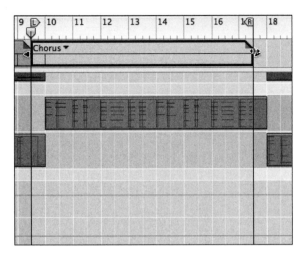

Figure 3.17 Tighten up the Chorus 1 Block.
Source: Propellerhead Software.

4. Proceed with making additional Blocks that envelope each section of the song. Label each new Block with these names, beginning and ending with these measures.
Labels and Measures laid out:

▷ Verse 1—1.3 to 9.3
▷ Chorus 1—9.3 to 17.3
▷ Verse 2—17.3 to 25.3
▷ Chorus 2—25.3 to 34.1
▷ Bridge—34.1 to 42.1
▷ Chorus 3—42.1 to 50.3
▷ Outro—50.3 to 54.3

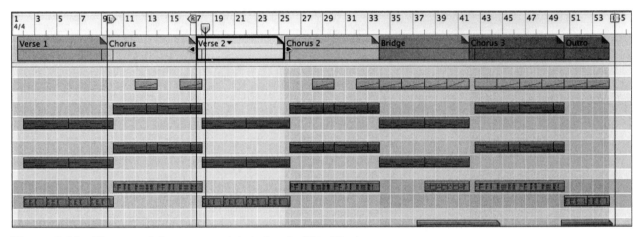

Figure 3.18 All parts of the song are labeled and within Blocks.
Source: Propellerhead Software.

5. Okay, now for some slicing and dicing! We're going to use the Razor tool in Reason to cut up the clips within Olivia's sequence so that we can easily separate out the main parts of the song and place them into Blocks. Press R to enable the Razor tool (see Figure 3.19).

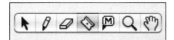

Figure 3.19 The Razor tool.
Source: Propellerhead Software.

6. Now, using the Razor tool, drag a square around the whole section of clips that correspond within the Verse 1 Block that you set up at the top (see Figure 3.20).

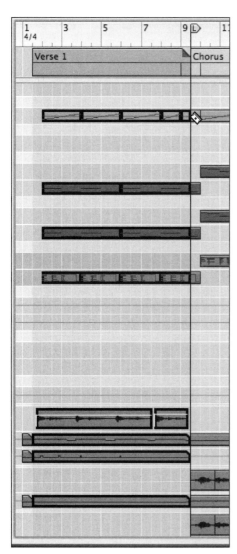

Figure 3.20 Drag-select with the Razor tool.
Source: Propellerhead Software.

7. Once you have used the Razor tool to separate clips that extend into Chorus 1, the tool will leave all the clips within the Verse 1 area highlighted. Hold down Cmd or Ctrl and press C. You may also use Edit → Copy (see Figure 3.21).

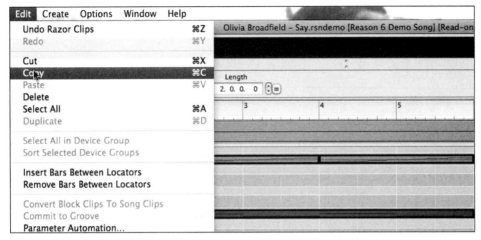

Figure 3.21 Copy selected within the Edit menu.
Source: Propellerhead Software.

8. Once you've copied the clips, double-click on Verse 1 Block. This will take you inside the Verse 1 Block (see Figure 3.22).

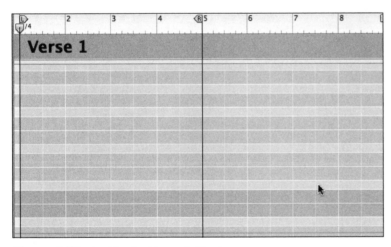

Figure 3.22 Inside the Verse 1 Block.
Source: Propellerhead Software.

9. Make sure that the Song Position pointer is at measure 1 within the Block; then hold down the Cmd/Ctrl button and press V. This will paste the clips into this Block (see Figure 3.23).

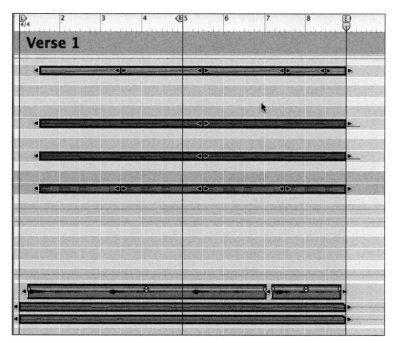

Figure 3.23 Clips pasted into the Verse 1 Block.
Source: Propellerhead Software.

10. Now, we'll need to set up the loop points within the Verse 1 Block, so that it works in a way that's helpful and smooth as we go from part to part in the arrangement. Place the Left loop locator at measure 1 and the Right loop locator at measure 9. The E, or end marker, should be at measure 9, as well (see Figure 3.24).

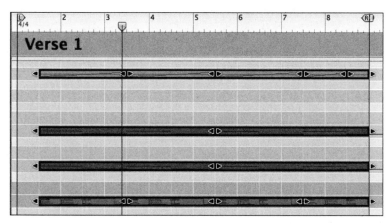

Figure 3.24 Placing loop points and the end marker.
Source: Propellerhead Software.

11. Press B and go back to Song mode (not shown).
12. Go ahead and repeat steps 6–10 with each section of the song. Essentially, you're Razor-selecting each section underneath each Block, copying each section into the corresponding Block above, and then setting up the loop points for each Block.

Smooth Blocks and How to Make Them

Some sections of the song may not transition in as smoothly as others. For example, Chorus 2 has a slight break before it starts up. I ended up placing my Left loop locator at measure 1.3 and my Right at measure 9.3 (see Figure 3.25). This is contrary to the fact that the section actually starts at measure 1. What this means is that when it's placed in the timeline, it will play the whole section but loop another section. And remember, this exercise is about fun, and it's the minor nuances, glitches, and mistakes that can really treat you to new tricks and give you new ideas.

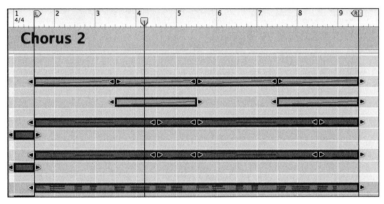

Figure 3.25 Loop markers at 1.3 and 9.3.
Source: Propellerhead Software.

13. Once all the sections of the song have been copied in to their corresponding Blocks, in Song mode, hold down Cmd/Ctrl and press A to highlight everything in the song (see Figure 3.26).

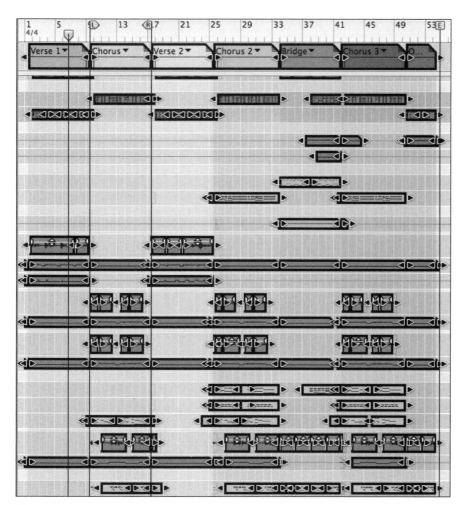

Figure 3.26 All the clips in the song selected with Cmd/Ctrl A.
Source: Propellerhead Software.

14. Press the Delete button (Backspace on a PC), and you'll wipe out everything in the song (see Figure 3.27)! Don't worry though, because your Blocks will still retain all of the copied song data.

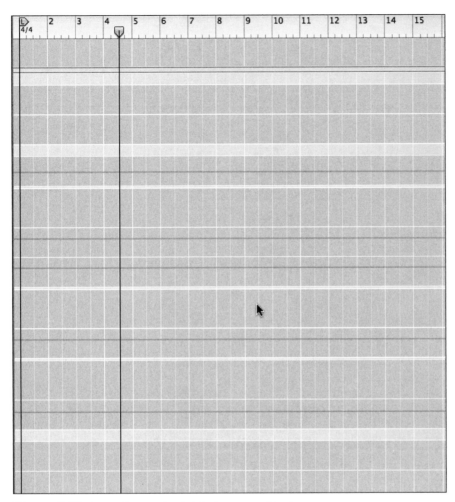

Figure 3.27 The aftermath of deleting everything!
Source: Propellerhead Software.

15. Now for the fun part! Draw in Blocks with the pencil tool at the top in the Blocks lane. To change to a different Block, click on the name and select another Block from the drop-down list. Choose any particular order. Have fun with different arrangements.

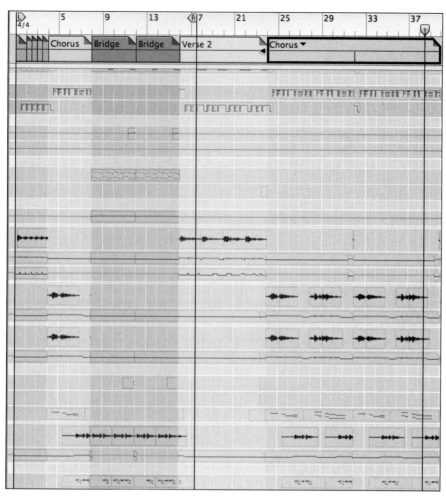

Figure 3.28 Painting in Blocks.
Source: Propellerhead Software.

Handlebars

If you click on a Block, you'll notice small handlebars, or arrows, appear next to the Block (see Figure 3.29). These indicate that you can resize from either the beginning or the end of the Block. So, if the Block doesn't start at exactly the right spot for you, size it so that it starts or ends where you want it. It doesn't have to play out to its full length.

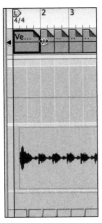

Figure 3.29 Notice how the selected clip has a triangular handlebar on the end of it.

Audio and Tempo

Also, remember that Reason automatically pitches and time shifts audio. In English, this means that if you change the tempo of the song, the audio changes in tempo, too. So the voice will speed up, slow down, etc. Try some different tempos. You can even use Tap Tempo to drum out a faster or slower beat. It is important to note that when you change the tempo, the pitch will not be altered (see Figure 3.30). So, don't worry about losing the original key.

Figure 3.30 Change the tempo in Reason.
Source: Propellerhead Software.

So, there you go, an easy setup remix palette that took very little effort. But, what's better is that with this palette of Blocks, with different song parts or sections, you can easily create arrangements that can be much more complex and intense than the original.

And we've really just scratched the surface. You can now start adding in instruments of your own that will in no way affect the existing instruments—because they are already set up in Blocks. We'll try this out now in the next exercise, so keep your work in this exercise available.

Easily Laying Down Drums for Remixes

You're no doubt looking at Reason in a whole new fashion. If you aren't, then either you have already progressed up to this point in your personal use of Reason, or you missed something in this chapter.

In this section, we're going to change the tempo, add in some drums, use a Redrum drum machine, and then break down the drums even further for easy mixing and producing.

Once you've set up Blocks, you should understand that what is not actually within each Block is technically separate. This means that once you have all of your basic elements within Blocks, it's very easy to start adding things over the top, while keeping the core elements intact.

Let me show you what I mean.

1. In the remix arrangement from the last exercise, create a Redrum drum machine (see Figure 3.31).

Figure 3.31 The Redrum drum machine.
Source: Propellerhead Software.

2. Load up the House Kit.drp into your Redrum drum machine (see Figure 3.32).

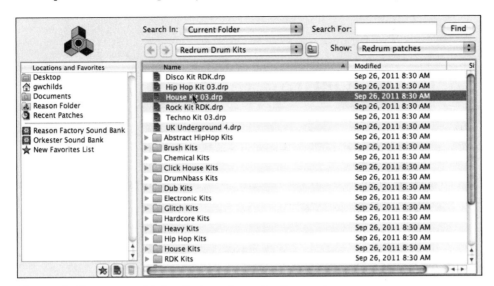

Figure 3.32 Select a kit for Redrum from the Reason browser.
Source: Propellerhead Software.

3. Channel 1 on the Redrum drum module will be selected by default. Draw in a beat on the 1, 5, 9, and 13 steps (see Figure 3.33).

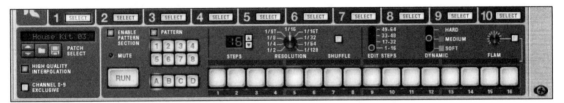

Figure 3.33 Create a kick pattern in Redrum.
Source: Propellerhead Software.

4. Select Channel 2 on the Redrum drum module (see Figure 3.34).

Figure 3.34 Channel 2 of Redrum.
Source: Propellerhead Software.

5. Click on steps 5 and 13 (see Figure 3.35).

Figure 3.35 Program a snare beat with Channel 2 of Redrum.
Source: Propellerhead Software.

Beat That Drum!

To hear the drumbeat in action, press the Run button, and don't worry about hearing it with your remix just yet.

6. Right-click on Redrum and select Copy Pattern. You can also simply hold down Cmd/Ctrl and press C (see Figure 3.36).

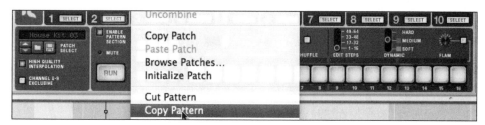

Figure 3.36 Copy a drum pattern in Redrum.
Source: Propellerhead Software.

7. Right-click on Redrum and select Paste Pattern. You can also simply hold down Cmd/Ctrl and press V (see Figure 3.37).

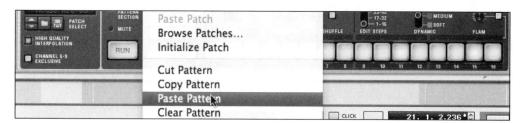

Figure 3.37 Paste a pattern in Redrum.
Source: Propellerhead Software.

8. Now, let's pick the tempo up just a hair, huh? Go ahead and adjust the tempo to 120 (see Figure 3.38).

Figure 3.38 Change the tempo in Reason.
Source: Propellerhead Software.

9. Select Channel 9 on the Redrum now and select steps 3, 7, 11, 15 (see Figure 3.39). This will add in a very generic open hi-hat. Don't worry, we'll get more intricate in a bit. What is kind of cool about this particular open hi-hat, though, is the little echo on the end of it. It gives a nice second shuffle at 120 BPM.

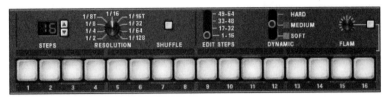

Figure 3.39 Program an open hi-hat.
Source: Propellerhead Software.

10. Now, let's add in some closed hi-hat with some nice tempo variations. Copy Pattern 2 to Pattern 3 using the directions outlined in steps 6 and 7. Then select Channel 8, which is the closed hi-hat for this kit. From here, click on steps 1, 5, 9 and 13 (see Figure 3.40) with the Dynamics switch set to Soft.

Figure 3.40 Set soft drum hits with the Dynamics switch.
Source: Propellerhead Software.

11. Next, select steps, 2, 4, 6, 8, 10, 12, 14, 16 in the Medium Dynamic setting (see Figure 3.41).

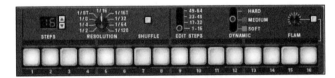

Figure 3.41 Set up the closed hi-hat with medium velocity dynamics.
Source: Propellerhead Software.

12. Then adjust the Velocity all the way up on Channel 8. This will really change up the dynamics in the hi-hat and help it groove a bit (see Figure 3.42).

Figure 3.42 Adjust the drum velocity of the closed hi-hat.
Source: Propellerhead Software.

13. Finally, let's make ourselves a snare roll that can be thrown into the song wherever we want. On Pattern 4, select Channel 2 again. Set the Resolution to 32nd notes as shown in Figure 3.43. Then draw in these steps in your Redrum with these dynamics (not shown).

   ▷ Steps 1–4, Soft Dynamics
   ▷ Steps 5–12, Medium Dynamics
   ▷ Steps 12–16, Hard Dynamics

Figure 3.43 Make a dynamic snare roll.
Source: Propellerhead Software.

14. Okay, we've got our patterns set up, so now we need to add them to the existing arrangement. Press F7 to go to the sequencer page (not shown).
15. While Redrum is selected and has MIDI focus, press the Create Pattern Lane button. This will automatically create a lane that automates pattern changes in Redrum (see Figure 3.44).

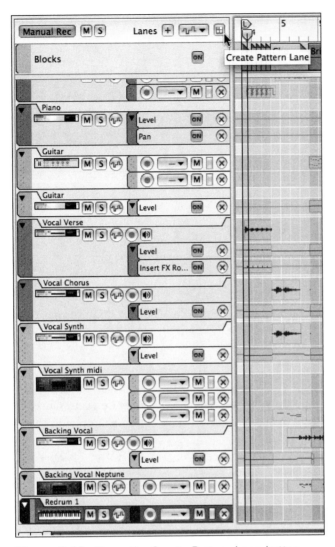

Figure 3.44 Press the Create Pattern Lane button.
Source: Propellerhead Software.

16. Draw in patterns now. This is done exactly the way you drew Blocks in the previous exercise. Try to make the drum patterns match up with the colored regions, with the exception of where you want the Pattern 4 drum break to appear (see Figures 3.45 and 3.46).

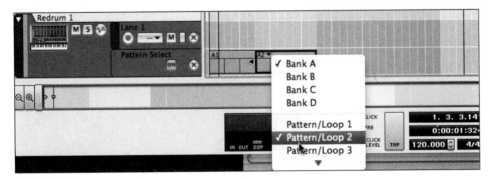

Figure 3.45 Draw in Redrum patterns into the sequencer.
Source: Propellerhead Software.

Figure 3.46 Draw in a break.
Source: Propellerhead Software.

Conclusion

You've added drums easily to remix. There was hardly any effort in that at all, right? All you had to do was create a few patterns and then draw them in, as if you were drawing in a coloring book.

However, there are a few things missing from this tutorial. We have the main drum patterns, but we don't have those minor fills, crashes, and so on that make the drums feel more authentic. That's where the next chapter is going to come in really handy.

We're going to take a look at the Tool window, which is chock-full of crazy MIDI editing functions, and we'll also get into some techniques for mixing down drums.

Deeper into Drums

I N THE LAST CHAPTER, we arranged with Blocks and also used pattern editing with Redrum. Through learning these functions, we discovered that it is relatively simple to arrange new tracks, but even more important, it's very simple to remix existing Reason songs. This is huge if you are either a producer, a remix producer, an audio engineer, or a composer, as you're able to label and move around parts of a song easily.

In this chapter, we're going to continue with the work that we did with Olivia Broadfield's track, and in doing so, get much deeper into the drums.

Turning a Weakness into a Strength

Seasoned producers tend to prefer to have utter control not only over the audio channels from drums but also the MIDI. This is where using drum patterns can be really irritating, because patterns hide the drum events and force you to create a new pattern for every basic nuance you want to add.

Thankfully, Propellerhead was aware of this and made it possible to easily convert any pattern into MIDI. Let's take a look at how to do this now.

Pattern Conversion to MIDI

Locate the Redrum track that you created and filled in the last exercise in Chapter 3. If you followed along through the entire exercise, you'll no doubt have drums arranged through most of the song, looking something like what's shown in Figure 4.1.

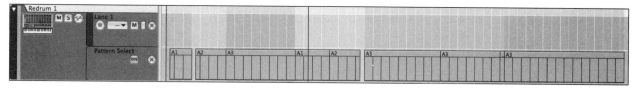

Figure 4.1 If you followed the last exercise, your Redrum track will look something like this.
Source: Propellerhead Software.

Let's convert all of these patterns into MIDI now.

1. Right-click on the track header of Redrum. This will cause the contextual menu to appear, as shown in Figure 4.2.

Figure 4.2 Right-click on the track header of Redrum.
Source: Propellerhead Software.

2. Select Convert Pattern Automation to Notes (see Figure 4.3).

Figure 4.3 Select Convert Pattern Automation to Notes.
Source: Propellerhead Software.

Immediately, what takes place is profound. Reason will automatically convert all of the patterns that were chained throughout the song into MIDI. This allows you to go in and add notes, edit notes, and so on, as shown in Figure 4.4.

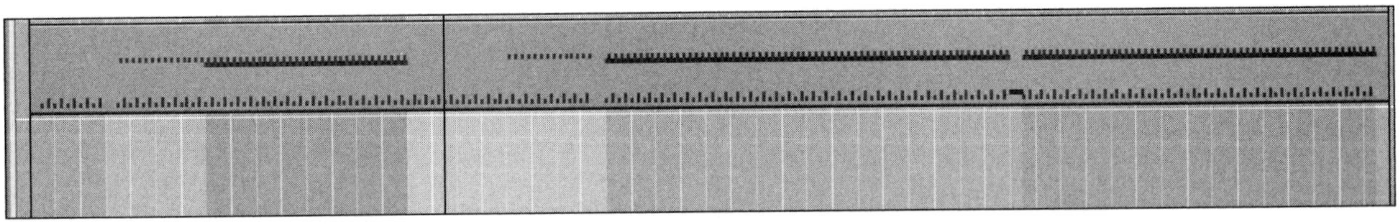

Figure 4.4 When you select Convert Pattern Automation to Notes, Reason converts all of the Pattern clips into MIDI clips.
Source: Propellerhead Software.

But what's even better is that the notes are still played exactly the same way they were before. Reason even takes care of Redrum for you by automatically turning the Pattern sequencer on Redrum off (see Figure 4.5). This keeps the Reason sequencer and the Pattern sequencer from playing on top of each other, which will create an ugly flanging double effect. You can always re-enable the Redrum Pattern sequencer again by going to the Redrum device in the rack and pressing the Enable Pattern section button on Redrum itself.

Figure 4.5 Reason will automatically disable the pattern section of the Redrum sequencer when your drum patterns are converted to MIDI.
Source: Propellerhead Software.

3. Because Reason gave you one giant part that is filled with all of your Redrum work, it might be nice to separate the part into smaller segments, in case you want to move the parts around, or if you feel like rearranging your Blocks later. (Optional) Press the R button to enable the Razor tool (see Figure 4.6).

Figure 4.6 Press the R button to enable the Razor tool.
Source: Propellerhead Software.

4. (Optional) Use the Razor tool now to chop up the sections of your drum clip (see Figure 4.7). If you'd prefer to keep the clip intact as one long clip, you can do so, of course. I only suggest this for people who might want further arrangements later.

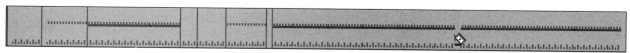

Figure 4.7 Use the Razor tool to divide up parts of the very long drum clip created by Reason.
Source: Propellerhead Software.

I'm sure you're thinking to yourself, "That was shockingly easy." And, in truth, it was. Some of the other applications out there definitely make you go through several steps with pattern devices, aside from third-party plug-ins that have drag-and-drop features. But even the drag-and-drop features do not automatically plot each pattern out for you. This truly is a feature unique to Reason. Keep in mind, this also works on other devices like Matrix and Dr. Rex.

Now, let's take it a step further. Most songwriters, producers, and engineers generally prefer having their drums on separate tracks, whether they are MIDI or not. And you may have already been considering using several instances of Redrum to create drums on multiple tracks. Actually, you don't need to do this. You can actually split all the drum parts up using the patterns we made and in the drum clips we used recently. Let's see how to do this.

Splitting Up Drums Parts into Separate MIDI Clips and Tracks

Most producers really like to have all the drums, whether they are MIDI or audio, separated on several tracks so that they can see and hear what the parts are doing. This also allows you to go in and delete certain instances of a snare, without tampering with what the bass drum is doing. Reason can do this easily.

1. Drag-select all the clips that you separated out from the last exercise (see Figure 4.8). If you did not follow the optional portions of the last exercise, just select the very large drum clip.

Figure 4.8 Select all the clips at once that you separated out from the last exercise.
Source: Propellerhead Software.

2. Press F8 to open up the Tool window, a floating window with several different pages. This is a very powerful window for MIDI editing, device selection, and also sequencing tools. Once you are within the Tool window, go to the Sequencer Tools page of the Tool window by pressing the Wrench button (see Figure 4.9).

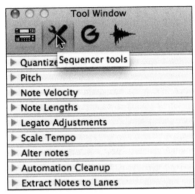

Figure 4.9 In the Tool window, select the Sequencer Tools page that has the Wrench icon.
Source: Propellerhead Software.

3. In the Tool window → Sequencer Tools Page, select the Extract Notes to Lanes section at the bottom of the sequencer page window. Simply press the arrow on the left to open up the section (see Figure 4.10).

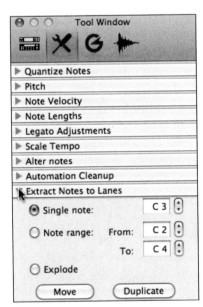

Figure 4.10 Open up the Extract Notes to Lanes section of the Tool window.
Source: Propellerhead Software.

4. In the Extract Notes to Lanes section, select the Explode function (see Figure 4.11). This whole section is used for separating MIDI out by notes. If you were doing musical parts, or just wanted to extract one drum, you

could use Single note or Note range. As these are drums, we want every possible drum that was used in Pattern mode to be given its own lane.

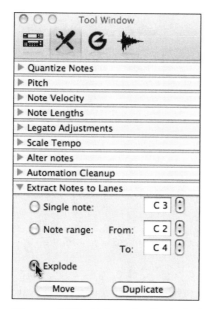

Figure 4.11 Select the Explode function in the Extract Notes to Lanes section of the Tool window.
Source: Propellerhead Software.

5. Now, here are two buttons you should know about, so when you use this function later in your own projects, you'll know what they mean.

   ▷ **Move:** This will convert all of the notes played (in this case drums) into separate lanes and clips, and delete the original clips that contained all of the drums.
   ▷ **Duplicate:** This will create separate clips with the drums in individual lanes (or notes) and keep the original clip containing all of the original drums.

I'm going to choose Move, as this will delete the original part, separate out all the drums, and is overall the best for minimizing screen real estate (see Figure 4.12).

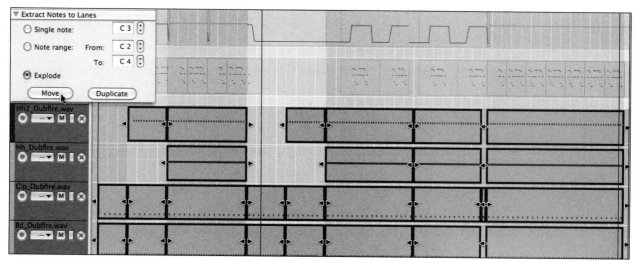

Figure 4.12 Press the Move button to convert the existing, selected clips into multiple, separated drums parts.
Source: Propellerhead Software.

6. If there is a part, once you've used the Explode function, that you don't want, don't worry. The drum lanes that are created can be removed easily by pressing the small X buttons on each lane, as shown in Figure 4.13.

Figure 4.13 Press the X buttons on the lanes that you do not want to keep.
Source: Propellerhead Software.

7. I also get rid of the Pattern Select Lane. Because everything is MIDI now, I no longer have need of it. Again, I press the X button to get rid of it (see Figure 4.14). Reason will, of course, tell you that there is data on this track. This is okay, just press Continue.

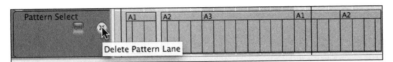

Figure 4.14 Delete the Pattern Select track by pushing the X button and then pressing Continue.
Source: Propellerhead Software.

8. As there were only four drums used in my Redrum patterns, I have only four drum tracks left. Regardless of the count that you or I have, it would be a good time to label each part. Double-click on the lane title to rename your drum part, as shown in Figure 4.15.

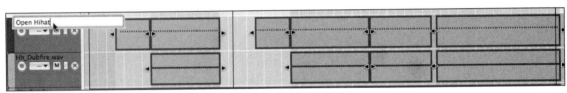

Figure 4.15 Double-click the current track title, which is currently the Redrum .wav file, and type in a basic name for your drum track.
Source: Propellerhead Software.

9. Proceed to label all parts so that you know what each drum lane is (see Figure 4.16). This will dramatically free up incessant soloing later.

Figure 4.16 Label all drum lanes.
Source: Propellerhead Software.

Now we have all of our drums that are being played by Redrum separated into separate MIDI tracks, but they are still contained neatly within the Redrum track and labeled. What's especially helpful by having our main drums all coming from Redrum is that the track can be condensed to free up screen real estate as well. Try pushing the arrow button next to Redrum 1 (which can also be relabeled), as shown in Figure 4.17.

Figure 4.17 Press the arrow next the Redrum 1 header to condense the track.
Source: Propellerhead Software.

Grouping

You'll notice that condensing the track down like this is highly reminiscent of other applications, especially when you set up group tracks. Reason does not currently have a way of grouping tracks. But by having drums, FX, and other tracks coming from one device, you still get a very similar effect. Granted, I'm not saying that it's okay not to have track grouping! But, if you're smart with how you set up certain devices within your song, you can achieve a very similar grouping type of behavior within your sequence lanes.

It's important to remember that Reason is designed in a way that each device can be pushed through the rack's signal flow to achieve multiple functions and multiple sounds at once through Control Voltages (found by pushing Tab behind each device) and through multiple audio outputs.

Let's take a look at setting up multiple outputs from a device and the benefits that go along with it.

Setting Up Multiple Audio Outputs for Drums

Now that we have all of our drums separated via MIDI, the obvious next step would be to set up multiple audio channels. This will allow you not only to control the levels and panning directly from the Reason mixer, but also to use individual effects on the drums. This will include the fine correctional effects within the Reason mixer, such as the following:

▷ Compression
▷ Gating
▷ EQ
▷ Filters
▷ Sidechaining

You'll also be able to set up multiple insert FX available in the Reason library and choose from individual Reason FX devices.

Continuing from the last exercise, let's take a look at how to do this now.

1. Press F6 to go to the Reason rack, as shown in Figure 4.18. We're going to need to do a little cabling to get this up and running.

Figure 4.18 Press F6 to access the Reason rack.
Source: Propellerhead Software.

2. Right-click underneath Redrum, which should be the last device in your Reason rack, to open up the contextual menu (see Figure 4.19).

Figure 4.19 Right-click to open the contextual menu.
Source: Propellerhead Software.

3. Choose Other → Mix Channel from the contextual menu. Mix Channels are exactly what they are titled, generic channels that allow a device to output a separate channel into the mixer. In the rack, they also act as container devices for the insert FX, and give you programming capabilities for the insert FX, so that you have access to favorite knobs while you're working in the mixer. We'll get more to that later. For the time being, create the Mix Channel (see Figure 4.20).

Figure 4.20 Choose Other → Mix Channel.
Source: Propellerhead Software.

4. OK, now we have a blank, unused Mix Channel sitting in the rack. This is where I can show you a handy trick. Hold the Option/Alt button, and then click and drag the Mix Channel down to the lower area of the rack. You'll notice that the original stays in place, and that you are dragging a duplicate (see Figure 4.21).

Figure 4.21 Option/Alt-drag your Mix Channel down to duplicate it.
Source: Propellerhead Software.

5. Next, do it two more times, or more, if you have more than four drum lanes from the last exercise. When you have as many Mix Channels as you have drum lanes from Redrum, stop. Remember: You can also Shift-select two Mix Channels and then Option-drag, or Alt-drag, to create two more at once (see Figure 4.22).

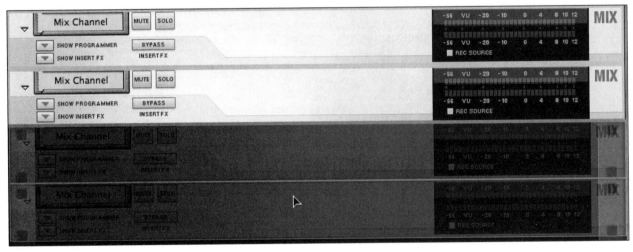

Figure 4.22 Create two, or more, drum channels again with Option- or Alt-drag.
Source: Propellerhead Software.

The trick here is that the only time Reason will allow you to Option-drag these devices without duplicating several other devices is when the Mix Channels are not technically hooked to anything. Also, the alternative to drag-duplication is to access the contextual menu, or Create menu, over and over again, which can be very tedious if you need multiple Mix Channels. Currently, Reason has a key command for rapidly creating audio tracks but not Mix Channels. This is a great way to speed up the process.

Alright, now we have several floating Mix Channels doing nothing. Let's rectify this situation.

6. Press F6 and F7 at the same time. This causes the Reason rack and the sequencer to appear at once (see Figure 4.23), which will help out in showing which drum comes out of each output.

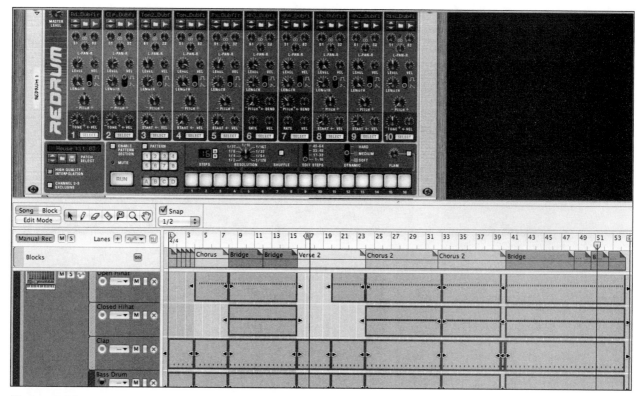

Figure 4.23 Press F6 and F7 to see the sequencer and rack page all at once.
Source: Propellerhead Software.

7. Play a part of your song where all the drums play at once. This will show you what channels are being used on Redrum because the lights at the top will go off each time a part is played (see Figure 4.24). Granted, we could have noted the names before labeling in the last exercise, but most people forget to do that. In this case, I thought it would be nice to see the work-around, in case you forgot. It may appear that I have fewer than four, but it's hard to take a screen capture of real-time drums.

Figure 4.24 Play your song while watching the lights at the top of Reason to see which channels to use.
Source: Propellerhead Software.

8. I've noted that 1, 2, 8, 9 are the drum channels I'll need to route. Depending on which drums you used when creating your patterns, you may have different numbers. This is no big deal. Now, press the Tab button to turn your rack around (see Figure 4.25). We need to route some cables now. You may also want to press F6, so that only the rack is showing. It helps to be able to see more.

Figure 4.25 Press the Tab button so that you have access to the Redrum Outputs and press F6, so that only the rack is showing.
Source: Propellerhead Software.

9. Now, drag cables from your first output. In my case, this is Channel 1 going from my Redrum device. I'll drag this into the Input section of the first Mix Channel shown in Figure 4.26. Make sure that you drag the Left Output from the Redrum to the Left Output of the Mix Channel. This will cause the Right cable to appear automatically. If you do Right to Right, you'll have to manually take care of the Left channel.

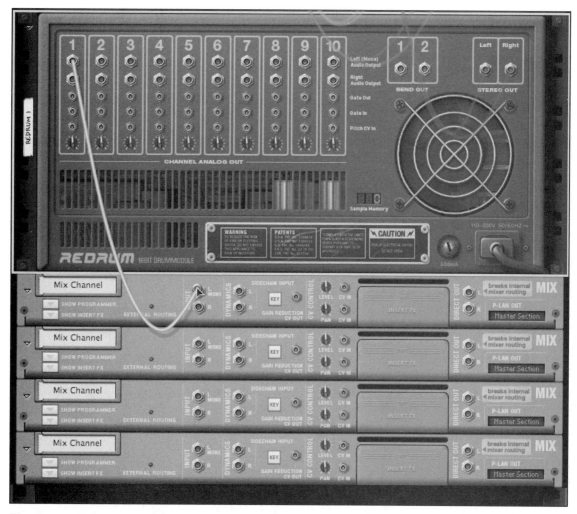

Figure 4.26 Drag a cable from your first output to the Mix Channel Input.
Source: Propellerhead Software.

10. You'll notice that your Mix Channel will automatically be renamed, as soon as you route cables into the Mix Channels Input. I am going to actually rename this with my own title, so I recognize it easily. I would recommend that you use the same labels that were used in the last exercise, where we labeled each drum lane (see Figure 4.27).

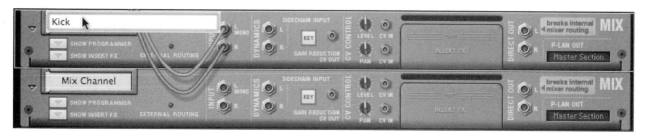

Figure 4.27 Click on the Mix Channel Label and type in a label.
Source: Propellerhead Software.

11. Repeat these last two steps for each Redrum and Mix Channel (see Figure 4.28). Remember, Left Redrum Output to Left Mix Channel Input.

Figure 4.28 Connect the remaining cables and label the remaining devices.
Source: Propellerhead Software.

12. Press F5 to go to the Mix Channel when you're finished. In Figure 4.29, you'll see your new drum channels neatly lined up and labeled.

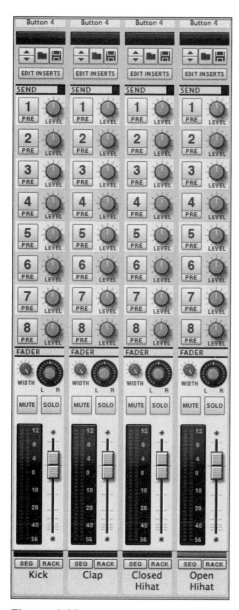

Figure 4.29 Press F5 to go to the Mix Channel and see your handiwork.
Source: Propellerhead Software.

Now you have full access to each drum channel while you're mixing your song. Also, your drums have access to all of the goodness that the Reason mixer provides. Remember: The Reason mixer is based on and functions very similarly to one of the most famous SSL boards out there—however, that costs far more money than Reason!

A Note About Mixer Grouping

You'll notice in Figure 4.29 that all of our drum channels have the same label color in the mixer. This is a byproduct of copying the initial Mix Channel at the beginning of this tutorial. Because Reason has no grouping system for Mix Channels, audio channels, etc., it's extremely helpful to keep your tracks color coded. This trick of Option-dragging (Alt-dragging) a Mix Channel to copy it for several outputs handles the colors for you ahead of time and gives you a quick visual reference for what color is grouped with what instrument.

Also, because we set all of our drums for this remix from one device, as mentioned earlier, we actually have the drums grouped in the sequencer as well. This is not the same as actually having a grouping feature, but it does handle it until Propellerhead adds one in.

Each drum channel, as mentioned earlier, can also have its own insert FX. Let's start exploring how to set up insert FX and how to program their knobs so that you have access to them from the Mix page.

Setting Up and Controlling Insert FX from the Mix Channel

The Mix Channels and the Audio Track devices are much more advanced than they appear. Or, an even better way of putting it would be that the audio channels in Reason are as advanced as you want them to be.

In truth, they are close cousins to the Reason oddity known as the Combinator. This is a device that can either be an instrument or an effect. It really just depends on what you fill it with and how you configure it.

The Mix Channel can be filled with devices as well, and these devices can be programmed to work in conjunction with one another in many different ways. But where the Combinator combines devices for almost any audio purpose that you can imagine, the Mix Channels and audio channels hold devices that are intended to be insert effects that only affect the channel they are combined with.

Even with all the explanation earlier, this may seem confusing. However, I think the added explanation will be appreciated once you complete the following exercise.

Adding an Insert Effect to a Mix Channel and Programming the Rotaries for Console Access

Let's put a simple reverb device as an insert on the Mix Channel that is associated with the Clap, in my case. You may choose another drum sound, but stay with the reverb device shown in the exercise in order to maintain some congruency.

1. Press the F6 button to open up the Reason rack; then locate the Mix Channel of your choice. I will be choosing the Clap Mix Channel (see Figure 4.30).

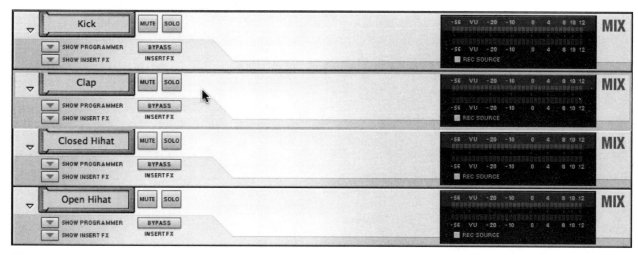

Figure 4.30 Press F6 and locate the Clap Mix Channel, or whichever device you want to add reverb to.
Source: Propellerhead Software.

2. Press the Show Insert FX button on your chosen Mix Channel, as shown in Figure 4.31.

Figure 4.31 Press the Show Insert FX button.
Source: Propellerhead Software.

3. A small black opening will appear underneath your chosen Mix Channel. Right-click in this area (see Figure 4.32). This will cause the contextual menu to appear. Also, a small red line will appear in the black area.

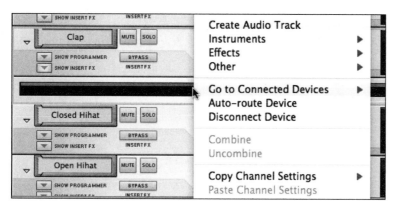

Figure 4.32 Right-click in the black area underneath the Mix Channel.
Source: Propellerhead Software.

4. Choose Effects → RV-7 Digital Reverb, as shown in Figure 4.33. You may be wondering why I'm choosing one of the older, smaller Reason reverbs. Actually, there is method to my madness. Reverbs use a lot of DSP, and we're already working in a demo that is highly populated. The RV-7 is actually the lesser of all of the reverb evils. So, I'll go with it, for the time being. If I decide to have a clap solo later in my remix, maybe I'll add a more elaborate effect.

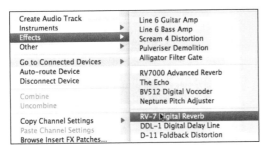

Figure 4.33 Choose the RV-7 Digital Reverb.
Source: Propellerhead Software.

5. Now that we have an effect in place, go ahead and listen for a moment. Notice how it works within the Mix Channel device with your clap or whatever you assigned it to. Try moving knobs around, too (see Figure 4.34). Also, try pressing the Tab button and looking at how the cables are connected. When you're done experimenting, move to step 6.

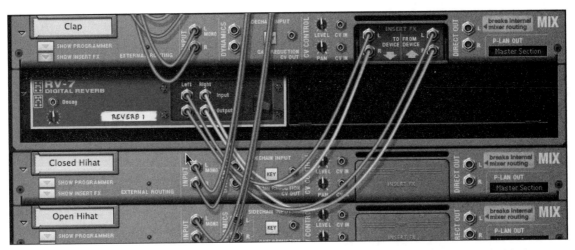

Figure 4.34 Experiment with the RV-7 Digital Reverb as an insert effect and notice how it's been routed into the Mix Channel.
Source: Propellerhead Software.

6. Now that you've had a little fun, let's try programming a knob. Press the Show Programmer button on the Mix Channel (see Figure 4.35).

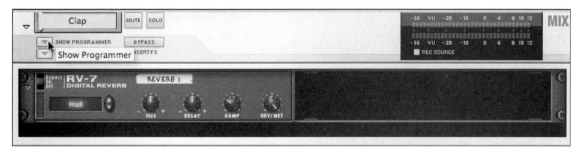

Figure 4.35 Press the Show Programmer on the Mix Channel.
Source: Propellerhead Software.

7. The Programmer can look a tad intimidating at first, to those of you who are unfamiliar with the Reason Combinator programmer. It's a piece of cake, really. You'll notice four knobs labeled generically, "Rotary 1-4", along with "Button 1-4". These do nothing until you program them to do something. Let's start on this now. Press the listing of Reverb 1 in the Programmer window (see Figure 4.36). This will cause all of the routing options to open up.

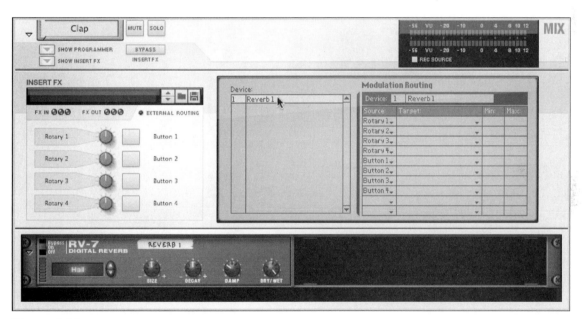

Figure 4.36 Select Reverb 1 listing in the Programmer window.
Source: Propellerhead Software.

8. With the Routing Option available, it's now time to set up some action. Assign Button 1's target to Enabled (see Figure 4.37). This will provide us with a way to turn off the reverb from the mixer, if we want to.

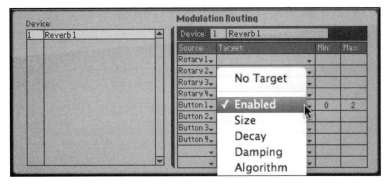

Figure 4.37 Choose Enabled as the Button 1 target.
Source: Propellerhead Software.

9. If you jumped ahead and tried Button 1 out, you'll have noticed that it currently causes the reverb to go from Bypass to Off. Not very handy, eh? Let's specify the switch movement. Set the Min (Minimum) number to 2 (see Figure 4.38). This will set the Reverb 1 to Bypass when the button is depressed. Set the Maximum to 1. This will cause the Reverb 1 unit to turn On when the button is pressed.

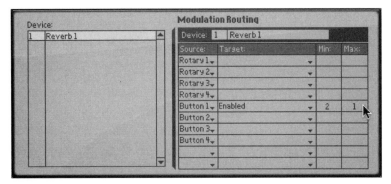

Figure 4.38 Set the Target Min to 2 and the Target Max to 1. This will set the button up properly.
Source: Propellerhead Software.

10. Now, just so that we know which button does what, let's label the button we've assigned. I'll click where it says Button 1 on the faceplate of the Mix Channel and type in Reverb On/Off (see Figure 4.39).

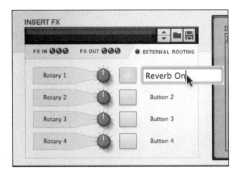

Figure 4.39 Click where it says Button 1 and change the label to Reverb On.
Source: Propellerhead Software.

11. Since we're familiar with the programming process now, let's set up a Rotary knob, too. Assign Rotary 1 to the Dry/Wet knob of the Reverb 1 unit. This will allow us to control how "wet" the clap is. We won't worry about the Dry/Wet Min and Max, we'll just let the knob take care of this one. Because that's what knobs are for, right? Label the Rotary Rev Dry/Wet (see Figure 4.40).

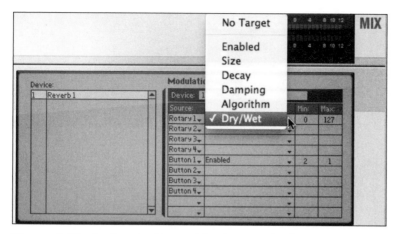

Figure 4.40 Assign the Rotary 1 knob to the Dry/Wet knob of the Reverb 1 unit.
Source: Propellerhead Software.

12. Finally, let's do one more Rotary—just for convenience. Assign Rotary 2 to the Decay knob on the front of the Reverb 1 unit (see Figure 4.41). Again, the Min and the Max are fine at -64 and 63. Your fingers can make the call on how much rotary you give in.

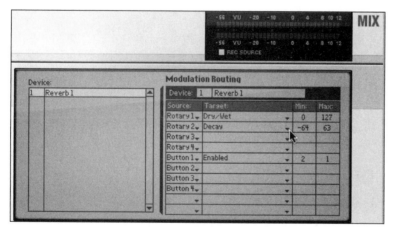

Figure 4.41 Set up Rotary 2 to control the Reverb 1 unit's decay knob.
Source: Propellerhead Software.

13. Okay, let's take a look at our handiwork. Press F5 to go to the Mixer page of Reason and locate the clap track or the track you chose to add the reverb as an insert to. You may need to scroll up to the Inserts section of the mixer to find your work. Once you're there, try pressing play and enjoy while you adjust your inserts without having to leave the Mixer window (see Figure 4.42). Notice that you have labels! Yes, labels in this huge mixer, there is order!

Figure 4.42 Notice the labeled knobs and control you have—one more reason you don't need to leave the Mixer window for your final mix.
Source: Propellerhead Software.

This feature has actually been glossed over heavily by many books, magazines, etc., but it really is a "must have" for serious producers and engineers. Keep in mind now that all of the drums we've used for this remix now have Mix Channels as well. This means you can load up on as many effects as you can handle. Before you move on to the next exercise, try adding in some more Insert effects on the other drum channels and see what you come up with.

Now that we've got the drums set up properly in the mixer and in the sequencer, let's add a little more. It's time to roll in some crashes and fills. Let's move on to the next exercise and see an easy way to knock this out.

Creating Easy Fills with Dub Tracks

Nothing spells out armchair drummer like drum parts that play repetitively without breaks or fills. And because we used Redrum's Pattern sequencer to create our drum parts originally, it might be time to throw in some fills and cymbals to make things a little more…real.

In this exercise, let's jump in and work through a quick and easy way to accomplish this with Dub tracks. Again, we'll be building off the work that we did with the Olivia Broadfield remix, so keep it around.

1. Select the Redrum lane that you created earlier in this chapter. Simply click on the picture of the Redrum device within the sequencer lane (see Figure 4.43). This will cause a keyboard to appear underneath the drum machine.

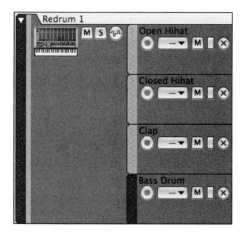

Figure 4.43 Verify that you have focused on the Redrum device by clicking on it and causing the keyboard to appear below.
Source: Propellerhead Software.

2. Now, let's create a new lane that will be expressly for our fills. Granted, fills are usually comprised of multiple drums and cymbals, depending on how you do them. This exercise takes this into account. We're going to throw our fills in one lane, and then we can explode them out later. Remember how easy it was? To create the lane, simply press the Dub button on the transport bar at the bottom, and a new lane will appear in your Redrum track area (see Figure 4.44). You can also push the , (comma) button on your keyboard to achieve this as well.

Figure 4.44 Press the Dub button on the transport bar to add an additional lane to the Redrum track area of the sequencer.
Source: Propellerhead Software.

Additional Lanes

There is another way to add lanes to a track within the sequencer. At the top of the sequencer window, in the upper-left hand corner, you'll notice a small area titled Lanes. If you press the + button in this area, another lane will appear in the same fashion that the Dub button creates a lane. The Alt button, next to the Dub button creates a lane as well, but it will mute every other lane within that instrument track. So use this function only when you're planning on having an Alt take of a track.

3. If you've been paying attention at all to the Redrum patch we're using currently, you'll notice that we have no crash. So let's amend this predicament by loading one up into the Redrum device. Press F6 to go to the rack (see Figure 4.45). Once you're there, press the Browse Sample button on Channel 10 of Redrum.

Figure 4.45 Press F6 to go to the Reason rack; then press the Browse Sample button on Channel 10 of the Redrum device.
Source: Propellerhead Software.

Channel 10

If you are presently using Channel 10 for one of your drum parts, you'll want to delete this lane in the Redrum track area.

4. You'll start off in the Rimshots folder of the Reason Factory Sound bank. This is because this patch previously used a rim shot on this channel. Press the Up One Folder button at the top of the browser, as shown in Figure 4.46. This will put you in the "xclusive drums sorted" folder.

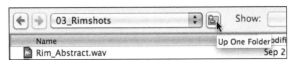

Figure 4.46 Press the Up One Folder button at the top of the Reason Browser.
Source: Propellerhead Software.

5. Double-click the Cymbals folder in the xclusive drums folder (not shown). Within this folder, locate Crash XTC5.wav. Double-click on it to select it (not shown). We now have our crash! If you were already using drum Channel 10 on Redrum, then you actually have a channel set up. If you weren't using Channel 10 at all, you'll notice that you have a track set up for 10 anyway. Even though it's not set up with its own Mix Channel. Redrum, as a device, actually has its main outputs set up already. What I will do is label the Redrum 1

Mix Channel device as Cymbals (see Figure 4.47). You, of course, can set up another Mix Channel for the cymbals, if you like. For the crash to sound like a crash, you'll also want to turn the Length knob all the way up on Channel 10 and put the Pitch knob in the middle.

Figure 4.47 Relabel the Redrum output as Cymbals (Optional).
Source: Propellerhead Software.

Channel Layouts

Channel layouts are very subjective and personal from producer to producer. Throughout this book, feel free to set up things to your standards. I tend to use my Cymbals channel as a sub-mix. The Redrum drum machine has panning and level controls, so I'll dial in my cymbal panning on the Redrum drum module. You may prefer to do this all from the mixer, and that's completely okay.

6. Next, I'll drag my cymbals output underneath Redrum, where it's with my other drum channels, within the rack. I'll also change the color of the Mix Channel to Light Olive, as this is the same color as the rest of my drum channels. I do this by right-clicking on the Mixer Channel, titled Cymbals, and selecting Change Track Color, at the bottom (see Figures 4.48 and 4.49).

Figure 4.48 Drag the Redrum channel, now titled Cymbals, down where the other drum channels are.
Source: Propellerhead Software.

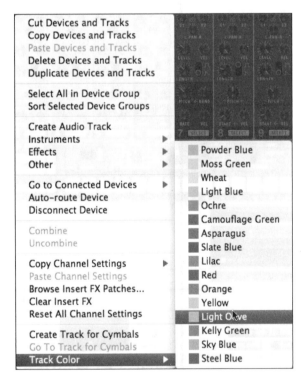

Figure 4.49 Now change the color.
Source: Propellerhead Software.

7. Now, return to the sequencer window by pressing F7. We are now ready to record some fills. Lane 5 will already be Record-ready, which is shown by having the red, track arm button lit up. Locate the crash on your MIDI controller and any other drums you want to record. Then, when you're ready, start recording. You'll have a dedicated lane to fills (see Figure 4.50).

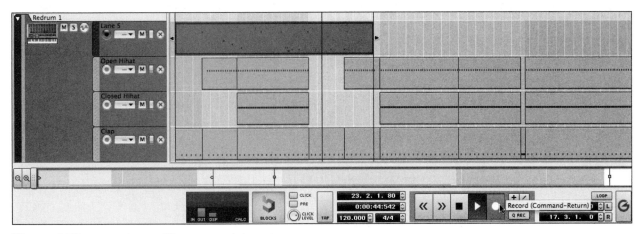

Figure 4.50 Record your fills, at your leisure!
Source: Propellerhead Software.

The great thing about having the fills on a separate lane, like this, is that you can free-form all you want on the drums and never have to worry about throwing any of your other tracks out of whack. Later, when you're finished recording, you can separate out the drums using the Extract Notes to Lanes function in the Tool window to create even more lanes. You can also drop lanes of the same drum onto lanes that correspond with that drum and then join them, using the Join command from the contextual menu.

Make sure to save the remix once you're finished.

Sidechaining in Reason for Drums

In earlier versions of Reason, sidechaining could be a little strange, largely due to all of the extra routing you had to do. In recent versions (version 6 on up), sidechaining has become dramatically simplified by the inclusion of a main mixer and mixing infrastructure that is built to support, and even encourage, sidechaining.

For example, if you press Tab and look behind the Mix Channels and Audio Track devices, you'll actually notice that there is a dedicated Sidechain Input (see Figure 4.51).

Figure 4.51 Notice the Sidechain Input section of the Mix Channel device.
Source: Propellerhead Software.

In this exercise, we're going to take a look at one of the simplest, yet most sought after, sidechain ventures, wherein, we'll start looking at sidechaining the kick to modulate the amplitude of other parts of the mix.

For this exercise, go ahead and create a new, blank Reason session.

1. Create a Redrum drum computer. Load up the patch House Kit 03, which is a default Redrum patch that can be found at the root of the Redrum patch folder (see Figure 4.52). You can also use the search function in the browser that we used in Chapter 2, "Song Creation Workflows in Reason."

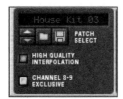

Figure 4.52 Load up the House Kit 03 patch in to the Redrum drum computer.
Source: Propellerhead Software.

2. Create a Dr. OctoRex Loop player (see Figure 4.53). We'll use this for a steady stream of percussion that will be modulated by the Kick drum.

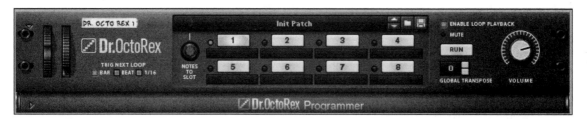

Figure 4.53 Create a Dr. OctoRex Loop player.
Source: Propellerhead Software.

3. Press the Browse Patch button on the Dr. OctoRex Loop player to open up the patch browser (see Figure 4.54).

Figure 4.54 Press the Browse Patch button on the Dr. OctoRex.
Source: Propellerhead Software.

4. Navigate to the Reason Factory Soundbank → Dr. OctoRex Patches → Drums → ElectroHouse → ElecHouse Tops Breaks 128.drex (see Figure 4.55). This is a great drum loop for the purposes of this exercise, in the sense that it will allow you to easily hear the sidechain modulation.

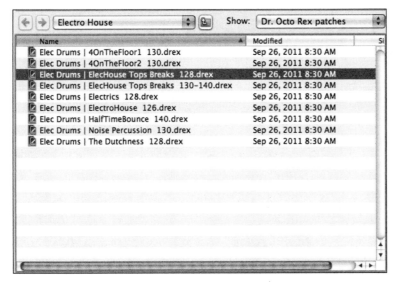

Figure 4.55 Locate the ElecHouse Tops Breaks 128.drex.
Source: Propellerhead Software.

5. On your Redrum drum computer, select Channel 1 and select steps 1, 5, 9, 13 (see Figure 4.56). This will give you a good ol' pounding kick drum to work with that can be your modulator.

Figure 4.56 Create a beat using Channel 1 on Redrum.
Source: Propellerhead Software.

6. Press the Play button now in Reason to hear what both devices sound like in context, before we start applying sidechain modulation. Just get a feel for how the loop drowns out the kick drum.
7. Now, press the Tab button to turn the rack around and navigate to the Mix Channel that is connecting the Redrum to the mixing console of Reason. Press the Show Insert FX button (see Figure 4.57).

Figure 4.57 Press the Show Insert FX button on the back of the Mix Channel device connected to the Redrum Drum Computer.
Source: Propellerhead Software.

8. You'll notice that when you opened up the device, the Insert FX panel In and Output section opened up as well. We'll use this opened section to set up a sidechain routing. Route the To Device Output from the Insert FX section into the Dynamics Input of the Dr. Octo Rex Mix Channel (see Figure 4.58).

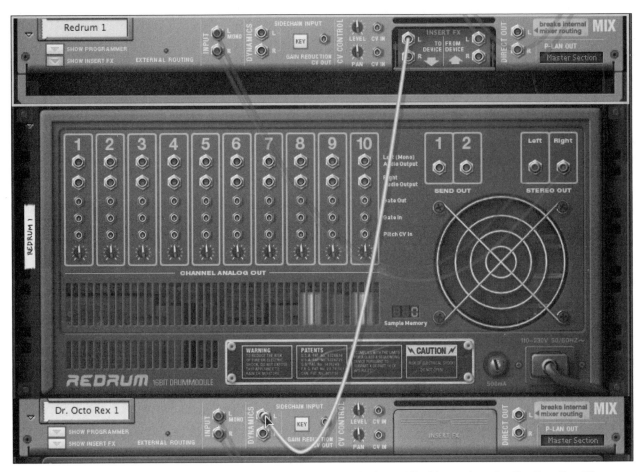

Figure 4.58 Drag a cable from the To Devices Output on the Redrum Mix Channel to the Dr. OctoRex Mix Channel, Dynamics Input.
Source: Propellerhead Software.

9. As soon as the cables are connected, the Key button will light up, letting you know that you now have sidechain activity. Go ahead and press the F5 button so that you can start tweaking the Mixer page. On the Mixer page, locate the Dynamics section of the Dr. OctoRex channel (see Figure 4.59).

Figure 4.59 Locate the Dynamics section of the Dr. OctoRex channel.
Source: Propellerhead Software.

Condensing the Mixer Channel

You'll notice that my Mixer Channel looks highly condensed. That's because it is. In the lower left-hand section of the Mixer page, you'll notice a row of buttons with abbreviations for several parts of the mixer. These buttons control which areas of the mixer are available for viewing and usage. As the mixer is so large, I'll often deselect parts that I'm not currently using so that I can get around much quicker to areas that I am using. Try them out. For this exercise, though, make sure you leave the Dynamics section open.

10. Press the spacebar to start your Dr. OctoRex and enable the Compressor by pressing the On button at the top of the Dynamics section (see Figure 4.60).

Figure 4.60 Enable the Compressor!
Source: Propellerhead Software.

11. We're going to resort to extreme compression so that we can actually hear what's taking place. Later, you can go back and adjust your compression settings to taste. Turn the Threshold (Thres) down all the way (see Figure 4.61).

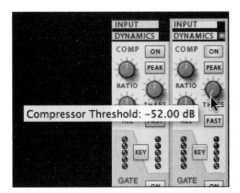

Figure 4.61 Turn the Threshold knob down all the way.
Source: Propellerhead Software.

12. Turn the Ratio knob all the way up (see Figure 4.62). Let's leave no room for doubt!

Figure 4.62 Up your Compressor Ratio all the way.
Source: Propellerhead Software.

13. Now, you should be hearing the sidechain compression. You're now getting the pushing effect that is prevalent in many dance music tracks. If you're not sure that you are hearing the modulation effect, press the Key button and listen to the difference with sidechain modulation off (see Figure 4.63).

Figure 4.63 Press the Key button to disable sidechain modulation so that you can hear the difference.
Source: Propellerhead Software.

14. Try adjusting the Release (Rel) knob to tighten or loosen the tail of the loop as it pushes in (see Figure 4.64). You'll notice that it becomes tighter when you increase the Release knob all the way. But, remember, this behavior can vary greatly, depending on the loop and the kick drum you're using to modulate the loop, or whatever else you're modulating.

Figure 4.64 Adjust the Rel knob to tighten and loosen the pushing of the sidechain modulation.
Source: Propellerhead Software.

Conclusion

There you have it, sidechaining made easy! Keep in mind, there are several other methods that we'll be exploring as we work our way through this book. Most notably in Chapter 6, "Cords and Combinators," where we'll get into working more with Reason's tools for vocals.

Keep in mind that when sidechaining is enabled, the gate is also being affected. The gate can really help you go farther in sculpting the track that is being modulated by cutting out certain parts. I highly recommend playing with this by using the loop and the kick drum in the current exercise scenario.

Okay, we've gotten heavy into techniques that can make life much easier for drum production in this chapter. In the next chapter, we're going to be exploring the ability to sample drums and several other types of instruments.

Sampling in Reason

S AMPLING IS A METHOD that is highly used, yet sorely missed, in many modern music applications. Why do I say *missed*? Well, back in the 1980s and 1990s, the sampler was considered to be the centerpiece of any collection of gear. This was mainly because it could do something that no other instrument could do: It could play back recorded, digital audio melodically through easy triggers, like a keyboard or a pad trigger.

As sampling instruments became more powerful and more complicated, the instruments that they were playing back became more powerful and complicated as well. Eventually, they were being used in place of elaborate orchestras and expensive instruments that were for all intents and purposes, unattainable. Ever try buying a Stradivarius?

Now, in modern music, sampling instruments are still around, but are often stand-alone items that must be purchased in addition to your DAW. And then you get to buy the sample libraries.

This is where Reason is a serious exception.

Reason's sampling capability is actually on par, and in some ways more advanced, than even the most intense sampling instruments out there. And because of devices like the Combinator (see Chapter 6, "Cords and Combinators"), you can create highly authentic and elaborate instruments of your own by combining many of Reason's sampling instruments.

But there's one more reason that the sampling instruments in Reason remain powerful and different in comparison to other software applications: You can sample in the same fashion as you used to on your old sampling keyboards, drum machines, and so on.

Reason truly does emulate hardware. So what are the sampling instruments?

Sampling Instruments in Reason

In Reason, you will find a few gems that are capable of not only sampling but also sampling playback. Look at Figure 5.1 and the capabilities marked therein.

Instrument	Capabilities	Description	Old School Equivalent
Redrum	Sampling, Sample Playback	Drum Machine/Drum Module	ASR-X
NN-XT	Sampling, Sample Playback, Velocity Mapping, Mappable, Elaborate Sample Patch Management	Sampler/Sample Playback Device	Akai S1000 and Higher
NN-19	Sampling, Sample Playback, Mappable, Some Map, Very Basic Sample Patch Management. Much lighter on processor.	Sampler/Sample Playback Device	Akai S900, and lower
Kong	Drum Module with Sampling Capabilities. Pad based.m Highly Editable.	Drum Module/ Loop Playback/ Cool Drum Pads	Akai MPC

Figure 5.1 This is a diagram of the instruments and their capabilities.
Source: Propellerhead Software.

Each instrument samples, and manages samples, in ways that match the instruments that inspired them. For example, the Kong Drum Module behaves very similarly to the working of a sampler from the Akai MPC line.

Is the art and functionality of each device just cosmetic and novel? Not really, because every device has a purpose in the grand scheme of Reason. Another example would be that the NN-19 Sampler is a lighter version (although the NN-19 was in Reason first) of the more elaborate NN-XT. If you don't need an elaborate sampler, and you just need a basic sample patch, then save your resources and use an NN-19.

Sampling Inputs and Reconfiguration Possibilities

Before we get into any of the individual instruments, let's take a look at how Reason samples, since it is very similar to the old-school devices you may have used back in the day.

Press the F6 button to bring up the Reason rack; then press the Tab button to turn the rack around. You'll notice that there are several inputs and outputs at the top of the page (see Figure 5.2).

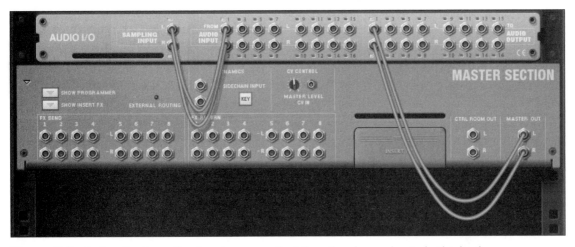

Figure 5.2 Notice the Sampling Input among all of the other ins and outs in the back.
Source: Propellerhead Software.

These inputs and outputs are how you configure multiple outputs and inputs on your audio interface and Rewire, which we'll get into in Chapter 7, "Effect Combinators: 2." To the far left, you'll notice the Sampling Input section of the hardware interface. When you route an input into the Sampling Input, you can record whatever is coming into your physical audio input and into the Reason Sampling Input.

Keep in mind, the input that is routed to the Sampling Input can still be accessed as a recording input, but you also get the additional capability of being able to quickly and easily record into any of the devices that sample.

To understand which device input is mapped to the default Inputs 1 and 2, you'll need to go to the Reason Preferences → Audio Page. If your audio interface is a built-in audio device, like Apple Core Audio, then you'll have either Built-in Mic or Built-in Input to choose from. External audio devices will have the Active Input Channels menus to choose from.

You can also route Reason devices into the Sampling Input as well. This allows you to make quick sample loops, sounds, and so on from Reason itself. This feature may seem trivial, but I assure you that you can generate a very elaborate loop/sound library with this function, if you use it accordingly. For example, what if you want to create a flute sound that doesn't work for your current project, but you'd like to hold on to it? Why don't you sample it?

Additionally, the Reason Sampling devices can read regular AIF and WAV files. This can be very handy, because many of the audio libraries available come in this format.

There is also one other device that does something very similar to sampling. Let's talk about this now, before we move forward.

A Note About Dr. Octo Rex

Despite appearances, Dr. Octo Rex isn't exactly a sampler or a sample playback device. In actuality, Dr. Octo Rex and Nurse Rex (found in Kong) play back a proprietary audio file format created by Propellerhead, known as a .Rex file.

In order to bring your own audio files into Dr. Octo Rex, you'll need to encode them in a program created by Propellerhead called *Recycle*. Sadly, this software is not included with Reason, but it is a worthy purchase if loops are your thing.

Remember that the loops that are being played back by Dr. Octo Rex are far more intricate than regular loops. For example, every Hit or Slice available in the loop will be mapped across your MIDI keyboard, so you can use the loop as a drum kit, as well as play it back in any tempo.

Now, let's get to the true samplers, but we'll be coming back to Dr. Octo Rex in Chapter 7.

Sampling and Editing

As we've been working steadily with Redrum up to this point, I thought it might be nice to finish up with its sampling ability and move out from there. Also, this is the easiest of the devices in Reason to sample with, so it's an ideal starting device.

Go ahead and set up a new Reason session with a Redrum Drum Module only and a microphone going into your audio interface or your built-in mic on your computer. If you are using an audio interface, verify that the input coming into Reason is the input going into the Sampling Input discussed earlier in this chapter.

Now that you have this environment set up, let's try sampling.

1. If your Redrum Drum Computer does not say Initialize Patch in the lower left-hand corner, you'll want to right-click on Redrum and select Reset Device (see Figure 5.3).

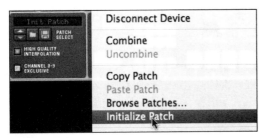

Figure 5.3 Verify that you're working with an initialized patch.
Source: Propellerhead Software.

2. Near the top of every Redrum channel, there are buttons that have a small waveform emblem. These are your sampling buttons. In many applications, you'll usually expect a menu to pop up and say something like, "You're about to begin sampling, etc." This is not the case with any of the Reason Sampling devices. When you press the Sampling button, you start recording, period. So, be ready. Now, for purposes of the exercise, I'd like you to make a bass drum type sound with your mouth, or thump a book, or do anything that would qualify as a bass drum. If you actually have a kick drum lying around...well, there you go. When you have a source, press the Sample button on Channel 1 (see Figure 5.4).

Figure 5.4 Press the Sample button and record a bass drum-like sound.
Source: Propellerhead Software.

3. Once you've pressed the Sample button, the Sampling window will appear, which is very distinct in the sense that there isn't really another window like it in all of Reason (see Figure 5.5). There are only two buttons here: Stop (the usual symbol for Stop: a square) and the Restart Sample button, which begins the recording anew. Press the Stop button when you are finished.

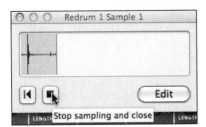

Figure 5.5 The Sample window in Reason.
Source: Propellerhead Software.

4. After you have recorded a sample you're satisfied with, it's time to fine-tune it. You can use the length, pitch, and other knobs to tighten up your sample, and also mold it to your specifications. However, I would highly

recommend doing a little bit of editing on your sample, as there will likely be space at the beginning, or it could be a little louder, and so on. Reason actually has a built-in Sample Editor of its own that is completely separate from the audio recording. Press F8 to bring up the Tools window and then select the Song Samples window, as shown in Figure 5.6.

Figure 5.6 Click the Song Samples window.
Source: Propellerhead Software.

5. In the Song Samples window, since recording, you'll notice that Redrum is listed in this window. If you click the small arrow next to Redrum, the samples that have been assigned to Redrum will be revealed. Select this single sample and press the Edit button at the bottom (see Figure 5.7).

Figure 5.7 Select your sample and press the Edit button.
Source: Propellerhead Software.

6. Welcome to the Reason Sample Editor. Believe it, or not, this is not a window that you hear people talking about very often in Reason conversations. However, it's very convenient, and it will really allow you to lock in your samples quickly and easily. The best part is that it works very similarly to all the other wave editors out there. Let's go ahead and tighten this recording up. Highlight the area of the recording you want to keep and press the Crop button (see Figure 5.8).

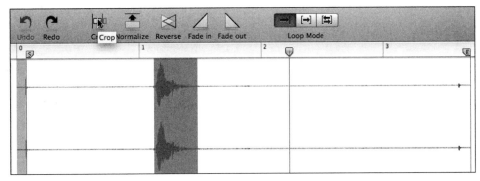

Figure 5.8 Highlight the area of the recording you want to hold onto and press the Crop button.
Source: Propellerhead Software.

7. Now we have a well-cropped sample that will definitely play back well in Redrum. At this point, I generally recommend doing an audio fadeout on the end of the sample, just to keep it clean. Try this now! Drag-select the end of the sample from where it starts to fade, up until the very end, and press Fade Out (see Figure 5.9). Remember: If you don't like your work, you can always use the Undo and Redo buttons in the left-hand corner of the Sample Editor.

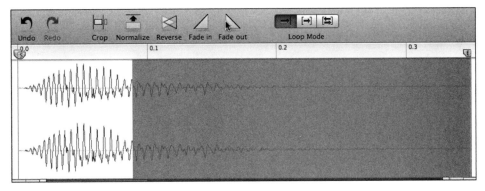

Figure 5.9 Select the end of your sample and press Fade Out.
Source: Propellerhead Software.

8. We have completed a basic sample editing task at this point. Now would be a good time to name and save your work. Type in a name for your sample in the lower left-hand corner of the sample editor; then press the Save button (see Figure 5.10).

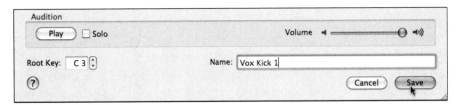

Figure 5.10 Type in a name for your sample and press the Save button.
Source: Propellerhead Software.

9. You'll notice that your sample appears with its new name within Redrum Channel 1. Also, because it's been cropped, faded, etc., it's much easier to work with. Try filling out a whole Redrum with samples on your own.

It's a load of fun, and you never know what kind of anarchy you can create. When you're done, we'll move on to sampling in a more advanced instrument in Reason and see how far you can go.

Velocity Mapping with Kong and Other Samplers

Kong does a lot, period. In the bowels of the beast, you will find remnants of technology that are dissected from every piece in Reason. Because it has a lighter version of the main sampler within Reason, the NN-XT, while at the same time being a hybrid of Redrum, is a logical instrument to move on to next.

In this exercise, I'd like to show you the next step in sampling: velocity mapping. This is where you'll assign the force in which you hit your MIDI controller with a specific sample. For example, if I were to hit the MIDI controller really softly, a sample of a light tap of a snare drum might play. If I hit the MIDI controller harder, a recording of the snare being hit very hard would play.

Velocity mapping allows you to create the semblance of very realistic instruments, because you are literally able to trigger different snapshots of different behaviors of the instrument you're trying to emulate. The exercise is designed not only to familiarize you with how all of the samplers in Reason velocity map, but also to give you a really good idea of how the innards of Kong work together. It really is a beast!

1. Create a Kong Drum Designer. If you have the Load Default Devices checked in Preferences → General, make sure you right-click on Kong and select Initialize Patch (see Figure 5.11). This will clear out all sounds, as you've noted in many other exercises.

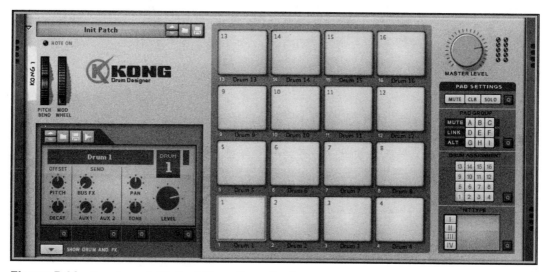

Figure 5.11 Create an initialized Kong Drum Designer.
Source: Propellerhead Software.

2. Now, press the Show Drum and FX button. This will open up the Drum Module area of Kong (see Figure 5.12). Kong is actually semi-modular, much the way that Thor the synthesizer is within Reason. There is an insane number of different types of modules that you can pick and choose from when making a percussion arrangement.

Figure 5.12 Press the Show Drum and FX button to open the Kong module area.
Source: Propellerhead Software.

3. This module area of Kong can be misleading at first, if you haven't worked with it before. You might immediately assume that this area is for every drum pad with Kong, but this area actually changes from pad to pad. For example, when you press Pad 2, the module show will change to the module assigned to Pad 2, from what was displayed on Pad 1. Press Pad 1 now, and let's actually add a module. Next to the small On button in the largest blank area of the Drum Module area, click the small drop-down area and choose NN-Nano (see Figure 5.13). This places the sample module of Kong onto Pad 1, or whichever pad is highlighted in blue above.

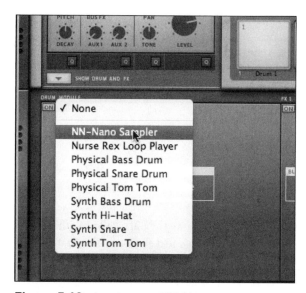

Figure 5.13 Load up an NN-Nano.
Source: Propellerhead Software.

4. Now, you've assigned the NN-Nano to Pad 1. This module may be small, but it is extremely powerful, and can be used several different ways. For this exercise, we're actually going to assign several samples to the NN-Nano. Let's start now. Push the Browse Sample button at the top of the NN-Nano, as shown in Figure 5.14.

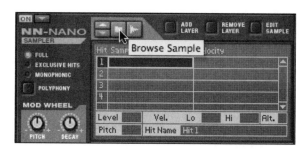

Figure 5.14 Press the Browse Sample button.
Source: Propellerhead Software.

5. Browse through the Reason Factory Sound Bank and locate the NN-XT Sampler Patches Folder → Drums and Percussion → Drums and Kits → Jazz Kit Samples (see Figure 5.15).

Figure 5.15 Navigate to the Jazz Kit Samples folder.
Source: Propellerhead Software.

6. Hold down the Shift button and select BD1 5 Jazz-L.wav through BD1 7 Jazz-L.wav (see Figure 5.16). Press the OK button at the bottom when you have them all selected.

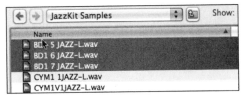

Figure 5.16 Shift-select all the BD1 Jazz samples.
Source: Propellerhead Software.

7. All of the BD1 samples have been loaded into the NN-Nano's first Hit, as they are called within Kong. Each Hit can be assigned to different pads within Kong. For the moment, let's just focus on the first Hit. In the first Hit, we have three different kick samples that audibly reproduce three stages of a kick drum being hit: Low, Medium, and High. You can demo each .wav file by holding down the Option/Alt button and then tapping the desired wave file (see Figure 5.17). You'll know you're doing it correctly when a small speaker icon appears while hovering over the sample. This can be extremely handy when you're configuring multi-samples within a layer. This also works the same with the NN-XT, which we're covering later in this chapter. (See the section in this chapter marked "NN-XT: The Sampler Powerhouse of Reason.")

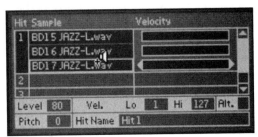

Figure 5.17 You can hold down Option or Alt and audition the samples within the NN-Nano.
Source: Propellerhead Software.

8. Now, let's actually do the velocity mapping. If you Option/Alt-click BD1 7 Jazz-L.wav, you'll hear a very slight kick drum hit. Now, click on it normally, by simply clicking on the sample layer normally so that only BD1 7 is highlighted. You'll notice that two arrows appear on either side of the velocity indicator. Slide the right arrow toward the left, and the Hi number will decrease. Move it until you reach 42 (see Figure 5.18). To slow the scrolling, or to get the number precise, hold down the Shift button while you move the right arrow.

Figure 5.18 Move the velocity slide from right to left.
Source: Propellerhead Software.

The MIDI Mapping of Kong

Kong is mapped across a MIDI keyboard controller in a manner that is very similar to most general MIDI drum patches. The pad we're editing in this exercise is actually mapped to C1, which is pretty standard for a kick drum in a General MIDI patch. Unlike general MIDI, Pad 1 is also mapped to C3.

9. For the next layer, we'll separate everything out again as another third. Let's adjust BD1 6 Jazz-L.wav's velocity settings to where Lo is set to 43 and Hi is set to 86 (see Figure 5.19). We'll use this sample as our medium velocity setting. If you press your controller with a medium intensity, this sample will play.

Figure 5.19 Adjust the Lo and Hi of BD1 6 Jazz-L.wav.
Source: Propellerhead Software.

10. Now, for the last sample. Adjust the topmost sample within our layer, so that Lo is now 87 and Hi is 127 (see Figure 5.20). With this setting in place, you can now hit this Pad, which is trigger-able on your controller with hard, soft, and medium, and the drum will play back in a manner that is realistic. Try different velocities on your own.

Figure 5.20 Adjust the Lo and Hi of BD1 5.Jazz-L.wav.
Source: Propellerhead Software.

Sample Pitch

For even added realism, or mere quirkiness, try adjusting the pitches for each sample as well (see Figure 5.21). This is a way to get a lot of character out of a single pad and make it much more expressive. What's awesome is that the pitch can be modified for each individual sample within the layer, in this case. So your low velocity kick sample (BD1 7) is pitched lower than the medium sample (BD1 8) and so on.

Figure 5.21 You can individually adjust the pitch for each sample within the layer.
Source: Propellerhead Software.

My personal preference with pitch is to use the Pitch section and the Pitch setting within the Velocity section of NN-Nano (see Figure 5.22). With the actual Pitch section, you adjust pitch bending in real time, as opposed to static changes introduced through some form of rendering. Within the Velocity section, it's even more interesting, as you can introduce pitch changes within all the samples, based on your velocities when triggering Pad 1. Pitch Bends and total pitch changes will take place as you play along, adding serious expressivity.

Figure 5.22 There are also real-time pitch possibilities within the NN-Nano.
Source: Propellerhead Software.

Now that we've explored working within one individual layer, let's take a look at working with multiple layers and how they can be used across Kong from one NN-Nano. Save your work because you're going to need it for the next exercise.

Using Multiple Hits from NN-Nano for Multi-Mapping

Now that we understand how one layer works within NN-Nano, it would be fitting to learn what having additional layers within one NN-Nano would achieve.

Like all samplers, you have the ability to map different keys to different samples. In the case of NN-Nano, you actually have the ability to map particular Hits to individual pads. In fact, you have to use Hits to map to multiple pads.

Let's try this out for demonstration purposes, and then we'll move on to seeing this in action with the NN-XT.

1. Click inside the Hit 2 default layer section of the NN-Nano programmer and then press the Browse Sample button (see Figure 5.23). Again, we're going to pillage the Reason Factory Sound Bank for more drum samples.

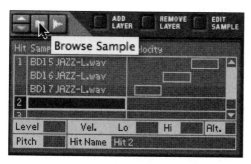

Figure 5.23 Press the Browse Sample button after selecting Hit 2's default layer.
Source: Propellerhead Software.

2. Locate and select the samples SN1 4 Jazz-L.wav through SN1 6 Jazz-L.wav (see Figure 5.24). Remember to use Shift to multi-select. Once you have these samples loaded into the NN-Nano on Hit 2, repeat the steps from the previous exercise for velocity mapping.

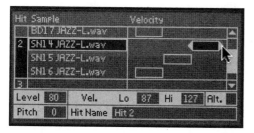

Figure 5.24 Load up SN1 6 through SN1 4 and velocity map these drum samples in the same way as the last exercise on Hit 2.
Source: Propellerhead Software.

3. Now, click on Pad 2, which is currently not assigned to anything. A blue square will appear around the pad. This merely informs you that the pad is selected (see Figure 5.25).

Figure 5.25 Press Pad 2 to select it.
Source: Propellerhead Software.

4. Once Pad 2 is selected, in the lower right-hand corner of the Kong interface, there is a grid with several numbers that represent the full number of pads present on Kong. Currently, you'll notice that Pad 2 is assigned to the Pad 2 module slot. Reassign Pad 2 to the Pad 1 module slot, that being the NN-Nano (see Figure 5.26).

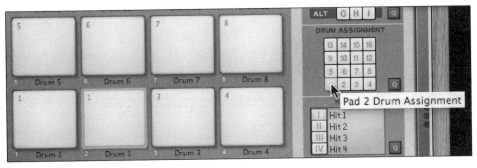

Figure 5.26 Assign Pad 2 to Pad 1.
Source: Propellerhead Software.

5. Finally, press Hit 2, which appears in the Hit Type window in the lower corner of the main Kong interface. This will assign Pad 2 to the velocity-mapped snare that you set up in the NN-Nano on Pad 1 (see Figure 5.27).

Figure 5.27 Assign Pad 2 to Hit 2.
Source: Propellerhead Software.

Hits in Kong are a unique way to allow all of your sample programming to reside in one programmer or a couple. This is far more effective than setting up multiple NN-Nanos on every pad on Kong, especially if they are all velocity mapped.

As you can tell, there can be 4 hits per NN-Nano. This means that 4 NN-Nanos can be set up for all 16 pads. Granted, you can set up an NN-Nano for each pad, but you will be switching around from programmer to programmer a total of 16 times. Why not consolidate your work and still have an awesome drum patch for Kong?

Let's take things a different direction with the work that we've done. The ability to create sample patches is a very big part of any studio production. But the ability to create loops and resample is a function that comes in handy for a myriad of reasons. For example, you might create a drum loop in the Reason sequencer that you'd like to keep around for future songs in the form of an audio loop. Or you might stack several instruments and want to resample all the work into a single audio file that can be played back in a sampler.

There are so many reasons to use resampling, and Reason really accommodates this need. Let's take a look at methods for doing this in the next exercise.

Converting Audio to Samples

Simply put, resampling is a way of bouncing current audio into a wave file that can be played back in either an audio track or a sampler. Every DAW actually has an audio export function or a bounce function. Reason actually has both, and between these functions and some of the sampler functions, you can easily start creating some really amazing sampler patches. These patches can be saved for future use, but it's also possible to create some really amazing sampler patches that can be most helpful if you're performing on stage as well—for example, triggering sampled backing vocals, guitar riffs, drum loops, sound bytes, and more.

In this exercise, let's take a look at how to set up such a sample patch with our current Kong patch in progress.

1. Click on Pad 1 (or Pad 2) to bring up our single NN-Nano. We still have a few Hits left, so why not make use of them, right? On Hit 3, browse within the current sample directory we've been working in (Jazz Kit Samples) for HH1 1 Jazz.wav. As this is just an exercise, I'm not going to require the velo-mapped hi-hat. But, if you would like to, feel free to use the rest of the HH1 series and velocity map to your heart's content.

2. Once you have the Hit 3 of your NN-Nano set up, go ahead and map Pad 3 to Drum 1 on the Drum Assignment matrix. Then assign Hit 3 to Pad 3. If you forgot how to do this, refer to the last exercise.

3. Now, let's get away from patch design and actually make some music. Using the snare, kick, and hi-hat pads that we've established over the last two exercises, create a drum loop in the sequencer. To do this, set up your left loop point at measure 1. Put your right loop locator at measure 3, as shown in Figure 5.28.

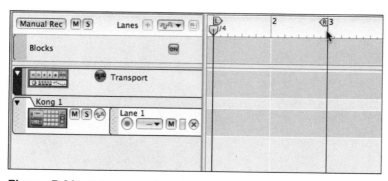

Figure 5.28 Set up your loop locators at measures 1 and 3.
Source: Propellerhead Software.

4. Once your locators are set up, record a drum loop in Loop mode (see Figure 5.29). (Press L on your keyboard or Loop on the transport bar at the bottom.) I would advise a drum loop that you might use on a regular basis. Who knows? You may end up saving this patch and using it several times later.

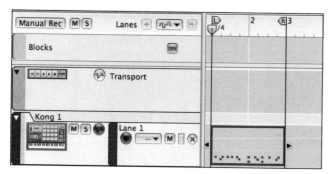

Figure 5.29 Record a drum loop in the sequencer.
Source: Propellerhead Software.

5. Once your drum loop is completed, go to the File menu and select Bounce Mixer Channels (see Figure 5.30). This is a way for you to convert your drums to audio without having to do some crazy loopback procedure. It's quick and clean.

Figure 5.30 Go to File → Bounce Mixer Channels.
Source: Propellerhead Software.

6. In the Bounce Mixer Channels menu, select Kong as your only Mixer Channel. Loop should be enabled. Also, make sure that Bounce to "New tracks in song" and "Mute original channels" are selected as well. Refer to Figure 5.31 if you need to.

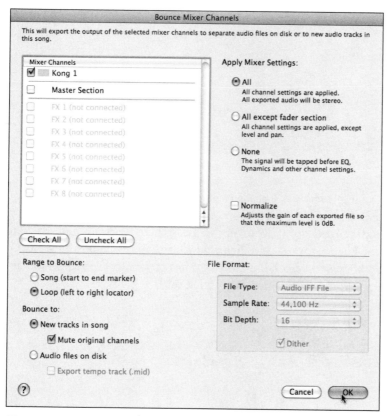

Figure 5.31 Make your Bounce Mixer Channels menu look like this one.
Source: Propellerhead Software.

7. Here is where it gets interesting. And, really, this is a feature I love in Reason. Again, the guys that make Reason prove that they are musicians as well. Right-click on your new audio clip in the sequencer and select Bounce Clips to New Samples (see Figure 5.32).

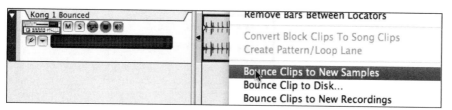

Figure 5.32 Right-click and select Bounce Clips to New Samples.
Source: Propellerhead Software.

8. Immediately, you'll see the Tools window appear on the Song Samples page. Within this page, you'll notice a new sample under Kong called Kong 1 Bounced. But it's important to note that Kong 1 Bounced is both generically named and sitting under Unassigned Samples. We'll need to rectify both situations. First, let's rectify the naming situation and do some light editing. Double-click on Kong 1 Bounced in the Tools window to bring up the editor (see Figure 5.33).

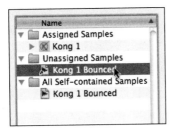

Figure 5.33 Double-click on Kong 1 Bounced in the Tools window.

Source: Propellerhead Software.

9. Beyond mere naming, we also have a sample loop that needs to actually be looped. If we were to drop it into Kong as-is, it would play as a one-shot sample. At the very top of the editor screen, under the Loop mode heading, there are the three Loop modes that Reason gives you: No Loop, Loop Forward, and Forward and Backward. Press the middle button for Loop Forward, and then title your sampled loop as Jazz Drum Loop 1. You'll also notice that there are Loop Markers in the Editor when Loop Forward is selected. Make sure that these Loop Markers are at the front and back of your loop (see Figure 5.34).

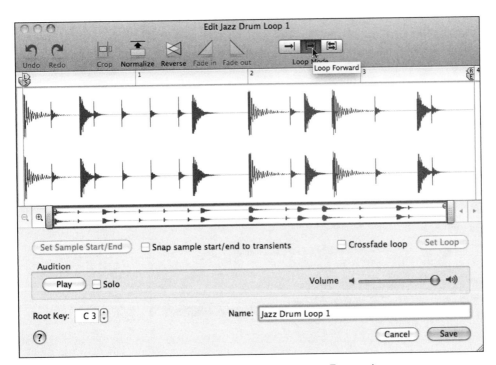

Figure 5.34 Name your loop and set its Loop mode to Forward.

Source: Propellerhead Software.

10. Now that the loop is labeled and actually looped in the editor, we need to assign it to a sample pad on Kong. We actually have one Hit left on the NN-Nano we've been using thus far. Let's make use of it. In the NN-Nano, scroll down until you see the single Hit 4 layer. Double-click within this layer to bring up the Reason browser. Once you're into the Reason browser, click on the Song Samples section listed within Locations and Favorites (see Figure 5.35).

Figure 5.35 Select Song Samples under Locations and Favorites.
Source: Propellerhead Software.

11. In this directory, we have access to every sample that is currently being used in this song. Furthermore, they are all categorized in a very straightforward way: Assigned Samples, Unassigned Samples, and All Self-Contained Samples. Go under the Unassigned Samples folder and choose Jazz Drum Loop 1 by double-clicking on it (see Figure 5.36).

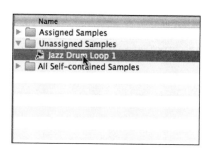

Figure 5.36 Double-click Jazz Drum Loop 1 in the Browser.
Source: Propellerhead Software.

Embedding Samples in Song Files

You should know that Reason has options for embedding samples within the actual song file. When you choose to embed samples through File → Self-Contain Settings, any loops or sounds you sample within Reason, or samples used from the Factory Sound Bank or a Refill, can be embedded into your actual song file (see Figure 5.37).

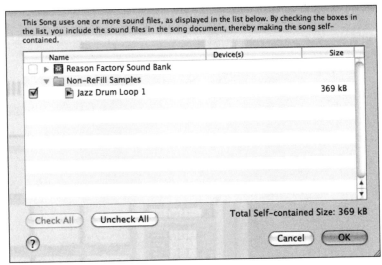

Figure 5.37 The Self-Contained Settings screen in Reason.

Source: Propellerhead Software.

If you are someone who collaborates with another Reason user somewhere else, you will love this. Why? For starters, if you're a sample maniac, you can embed your self-made samples in the song and your partner will have easy access to them when he opens your song file remotely. Secondly, there are loads of Refills (sound supplements for Reason) out there. You may have a Refill that your partner doesn't have. By embedding the samples, even if your partner does not have access to certain Refills you use, the samples will still be made available, and the song will play properly. Just make sure that you visit this section of the File menu before you send the song out! And, remember: The more samples you add, the bigger the song file gets. And this section does not include the actual audio files. Reason song files can get really large, but at least they are self-contained.

12. Assign Pad 4 to Drum 1 in the Drum Assignment matrix, like we did in the last exercise. Then assign Pad 4 to Hit 4 in the Hit Type menu (see Figure 5.38). And whatever you do—*don't press Pad 4 yet!* We have no way of toggling the loop off yet. If you press Pad 4, it will run constantly. We need to set up a Mute for it in the next step.

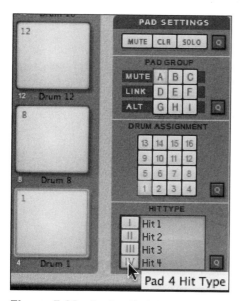

Figure 5.38 Assign Pad 4 to Drum 1 and the Pad 4 to Hit 4.
Source: Propellerhead Software.

13. We're going to use an unassigned pad now (Pad 5) to make a Mute for the looping Pad 4. If we don't do this, the loop we've created will play indefinitely with no way to stop it. With Pad 4 still highlighted in blue, select Mute: A under the Pad Group Matrix. Then click on Pad 5 and select Mute: A again under the Pad Group Matrix. You've just assigned Pad 5 to Mute Pad 4 when you want to stop the loop (see Figure 5.39). Give it a try.

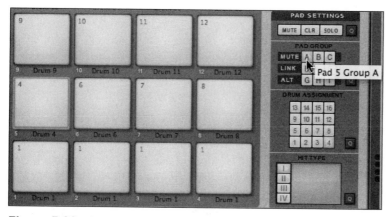

Figure 5.39 Set up Pad 5 to Mute Pad 4.
Source: Propellerhead Software.

Velocity and Pitch

You may notice that the loop is playing back at a faster pitch or rate than it had before. The last exercise mentioned the fact that you can assign Velocity to adjust the pitch of samples. While this feature is amazing for individual hits, make sure that the Pitch knob is set at 0% under the Velocity section of the NN-Nano (see Figure 5.40).

Figure 5.40 Make sure you have all Pitch features zeroed when using loops.

Source: Propellerhead Software.

It is also possible to adjust the polyphony of the NN-Nano to Exclusive Hits, or Monophonic, so that drums cancel out your loop. However, for demonstration purposes this patch will suffice. The big thing is that you know how to convert audio to samples, assign unassigned samples to a sample playback device, and the plethora of other topics this last exercise covered. You're now a sample master in Reason…almost. While Kong has a ton of sample capabilities under its hood, it doesn't come close to the NN-XT. Let's take a look at what else Reason has in the sample department.

NN-XT: The Sampler Powerhouse of Reason

As mentioned earlier, the NN-XT is the undisputed champion of all things sampling in Reason. The interesting thing is, though, the NN-Nano does a fair bit of all the basics, and has the exact same interface. The main difference is that the NN-XT does not limit you with sample layers, and it does not have Hits; it has groups. The groups are also unlimited in number per NN-XT within your songs. It can go very deep.

Another really fascinating feature of the NN-XT is that it has a fair bit of artificial intelligence in the sense that it will help you organize your key mappings through pitches. If you've ever worked with samplers in the past, and have attempted doing elaborate key mappings in an effort to build a realistic instrument, like a piano, you'll have discovered that it's not easy. In fact, it's seriously tedious. Having to individually map 52 keys of a piano is grueling, and it really takes the fun out of sample patch creation. The NN-XT did away with this, though. It makes this sad, tiresome process very simple. And, in this exercise, I'm going to show you how to take advantage of these amazing features, so that you can make some awesome patches of your own.

Tuning and Mapping a Real Instrument in the NN-XT

Rather than trying to sample an instrument together, I thought we could make it easier and utilize some of the raw work that Propellerhead has already done for us in the Reason Factory Sound bank. You'd actually be amazed at what you can find in terms of sample content when you look around in this expansive directory.

For this exercise, go ahead and create an NN-XT in a new Reason session. Confirm that the NN-XT is initialized. Also, a keyboard style MIDI controller with more than 25 keys is recommended for this exercise, as we'll be doing a melodic, realistic instrument.

Once you have everything set up, go ahead and proceed to step 1.

1. Press the small arrow button on the lower left-hand corner of the NN-XT to display the NN-XT Remote Editor (see Figure 5.41). You'll notice the similarities to the NN-Nano. This is where it all came from, though, not the reverse.

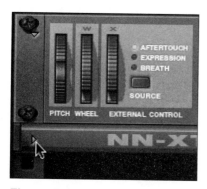

Figure 5.41 Open up the NN-XT Remote Editor.
Source: Propellerhead Software.

2. Once you're in the Remote Editor, right-click inside the blue screen of the editor to bring up the contextual menu and choose Browse Samples (see Figure 5.42).

Figure 5.42 Right-click in the blue editor window and choose Browse Samples.
Source: Propellerhead Software.

3. In the Reason browser, navigate to the Factory Sound Bank → NN-XT Sampler Patches → Piano → A Grand Piano Samples → ClPn2. This houses a very large directory of piano samples that is actually used for several piano patches that come in Reason. Rather than bringing up an existing NN-XT patch, we're going to create our own. Inside the ClPn2 folder, press Cmd/Ctrl-A to select every sample in the folder and press OK (see Figure 5.43).

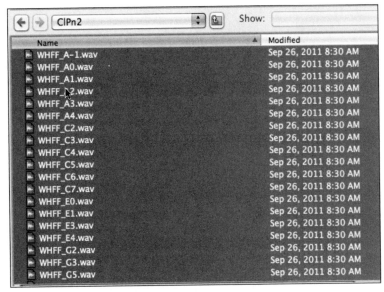

Figure 5.43 Select all the samples in the ClPn2 folder.
Source: Propellerhead Software.

4. We have a very large amount of samples to contend with now inside of the NN-XT. If you were to try to play the NN-XT right now, you'd notice a huge mess. In any other sampler, this could be an hour of work, with regard to setting all these samples up where they actually sound right. Let me show you how easy this is with the NN-XT. Right-click in the blue window now and choose Sort Zones by Note (see Figure 5.44). Now, all the notes are descending by key.

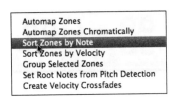

Figure 5.44 Sort Zones by Note.
Source: Propellerhead Software.

5. Now, let's have the NN-XT figure out the proper root note for each sample patch. Usually, just because a computer recorded a sound or tone, it still will not know the key in which it was played. Reason actually can discover it for you. Right-click and choose Set Root Notes from Pitch Detection, as shown in Figure 5.45. Each sample will be assigned a root note that matches the original recording. Yep, it works that fast.

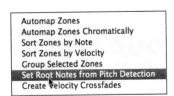

Figure 5.45 Set Root Notes from Pitch Detection.
Source: Propellerhead Software.

6. Here's where this gets really slick. You'll notice that all of the key zones are still overlapping. This causes every sample to play at once when a key is pressed. We need each sample mapped across the keyboard. Let's have Reason do it for us. Now that it knows the root notes for each sample, it actually can do the work. Right-click on the blue screen one last time and choose Automap Zones (see Figure 5.46). This will instantly cause Reason to map out each sample to the place where it belongs, instantly creating a fully mapped sample patch. Try it out!

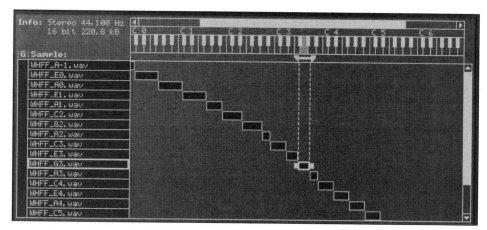

Figure 5.46 Reason maps out all the samples for you with Automap Zones.
Source: Propellerhead Software.

It's really that easy to have a fully tuned and mapped piano sample. What took forever before, now takes minutes. If you think about what this implies, it's stunning. You could literally record multiple piano samples out of order. Then, when you choose Set Root Notes from Pitch Detection, and then select Automap Zones, your work will be instantly mapped out for you. This is so much faster than how it used to be.

This makes it very easy for you to sample favorite instruments of your own, make patches of them, and then take them on the road. No sweat.

Conclusion

Reason has one of the most comprehensive series of samplers built into one tiny program. All of the capabilities that you wanted in the past are now right here at your fingertips. There are an infinite number of instruments, loop patches, and more that you can make easily for yourself, for live performances, and more. Try taking what you've learned through these exercises and coming up with some sample patches of your own. You'll be shocked at what's possible.

In the next chapter, we're going to start looking at the Combinator. This is a formidable device that does just about anything you want, through combining Reason devices. Once you start using it, I guarantee you, you won't ever want to put it down for long.

Cords and Combinators

6

THE LAST COUPLE OF CHAPTERS have predominantly dealt with the front panels of Reason. Admittedly, this area is the most attractive, as there are lots of colors, the knobs are there, and truly it is the main area that you use within the Reason rack.

This wouldn't be truly a Pro handbook if there weren't a great deal of time spent working behind the Reason rack, though. And I don't just mean routing audio cables; I'm also talking about Control Voltages. Every Reason device can actually be used for more than one purpose when Control Voltages are involved. For example, I can use the LFO of the Subtractor to modulate the Pan knob of the mixer.

If you feel a little intimidated by the concept of digging around behind a virtual rack of gear, plugging and unplugging virtual cords, you aren't alone! I have yet to meet a single producer, sound designer, or even engineer who doesn't blanch at the subject of working with Control Voltages in Reason. And it's not that the professional types whom I've mentioned can't handle Control Voltages. Actually, they are more than capable! It's just the time in learning that usually keeps them from it.

As you probably know, in most professional environments, when new software is brought in, it's all about getting the software working immediately. Many of the nuances that really let you explore and refine your ability with new software get left by the wayside because of important dates and milestones. If you (or your studio) fall into this category, I think you'll really enjoy this chapter. We're going to focus on exercises in the Combinator, which contains virtual racks of its own within the Reason rack.

Do you have to learn about Control Voltages to know Reason? Absolutely not! But you can really optimize your ability and the quality of patches you design and add fine nuances to your songs by taking advantage of them.

Control Voltages can get particularly intense when the Combinator is involved. Let's talk about the Combinator now.

The Power of the Combinator

The Combinator is neither an instrument nor an effect. It's actually an empty shell that holds several devices inside it. Through the use of knobs and buttons located on the front faceplate of the Combinator, you can control various devices contained within in any way that you desire through programming the knobs and buttons.

Because Reason has so many devices within it, a Combinator can become highly intricate, considering that you can mix and match so many different devices to form one amazingly complex instrument or effects device. It's all about what you're after.

You can actually create a marvelously intense Combinator patch without the use of Control Voltages as well. But, it's through the use of Control Voltages, and the amazing Combinator programmer, that you'll get those mind-blowing patches that will have everyone wondering how you did what you did.

Let's start by making a simple Combinator patch now.

Subtractor with Matrix in a Combinator

Two of the first devices to ever show their heads in Reason are the Subtractor synthesizer and the Matrix step sequencer. It makes sense, because they are classic devices that can form the core of any song you are working on.

For example, the Subtractor is capable of wonderful pads, leads, and effects. But it's particularly useful for solid, punch basses that can be synthesized with very little effort. When you couple the Subtractor with any step-sequencer like the Matrix, which is grid-based and simple, but capable of extremely intricate sequenced patches, well, you've got two devices that can easily form the core of your song melodies, if you let them.

The only problem with using both of these devices is that you often feel like you need more than two hands because there are so many buttons and knobs to press at once! This is where the Combinator comes in. You can program particular knobs and buttons to do multiple tasks at once. These knobs and buttons (four knobs, four buttons) are also assigned to actual hardware knobs and buttons (depending on your MIDI controller). This means that you can achieve control of several functions through the use of a few buttons and knobs that you physically have control of.

Let me show you what I mean:

1. In an empty Reason session, create a Subtractor synthesizer and a Matrix (see Figure 6.1). Make sure that you initialize the Subtractor synthesizer with the Reset Device function from the contextual menu, if it doesn't already say Init Patch.

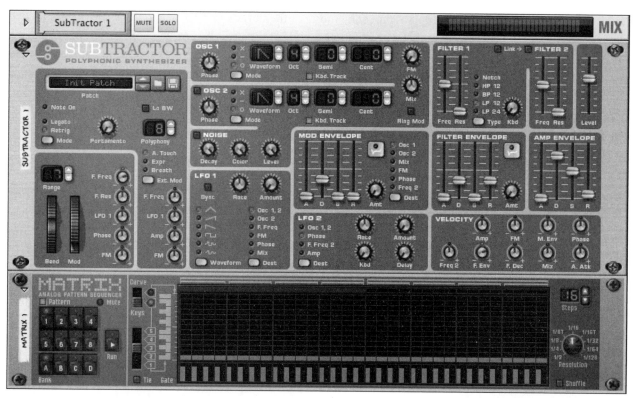

Figure 6.1 Create a Subtractor and a Matrix.
Source: Propellerhead Software.

2. Hold the Shift button and select both devices so that there is a blue field around both, as shown in Figure 6.2.

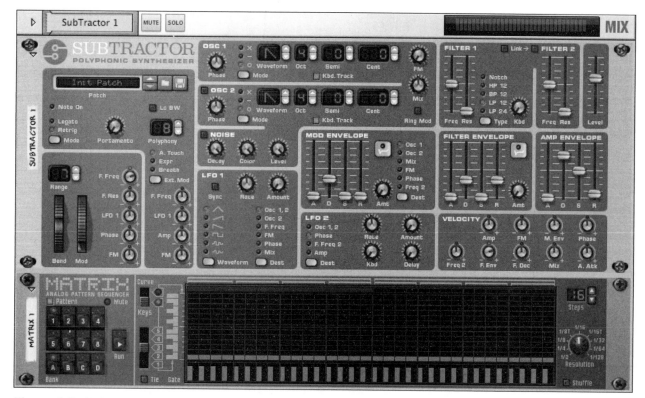

Figure 6.2 Hold down the Shift button and select multiple devices.
Source: Propellerhead Software.

3. With both devices now selected, right-click on one of the devices and select Combine (see Figure 6.3). This will automatically generate a Combinator device, and both devices will be carefully laid inside with their wiring intact. Press Tab to take a look.

Figure 6.3 Select Combine from the contextual menu.
Source: Propellerhead Software.

Mix Channels in the Mix

When you create new devices in the Reason rack, a Mix Channel will always be created for any device with an audio output. This can be confusing when using the Combine function to create a new Combinator. Reason is actually really smart about what it allows into a Combinator and what it doesn't. Simply select the devices you want in the Combinator, and when it comes time to combine, it will delete erroneous Mix Channels and audio tracks.

CV Tip: Sequencer Controls

You'll notice that inside the back of the newly created Combinator, you have some routing that has already taken place. This routing actually happened before we combined everything; the Reason elf/engineer is always working. Look at the patch cables going from the Matrix to the Subtractor. You'll notice that there are cables going from Gate CV on the Matrix to Gate under the Sequencer Control section of the Subtractor, which is shown in Figure 6.4. Gate in CV information controls Note On, Velocity, and Note Off information coming from the Matrix and going to the Subtractor.

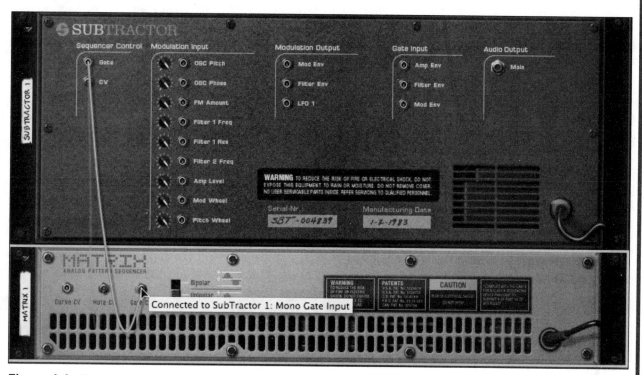

Figure 6.4 The Gate CV output of the Matrix going to the Gate input of the Subtractor.
Source: Propellerhead Software.

Matrix Note CV

You'll also notice that Note CV from the Matrix is going to CV under the Sequencer Control on the Subtractor as well (see Figure 6.5). Note CV is actually sending the note information from the Matrix to the Subtractor.

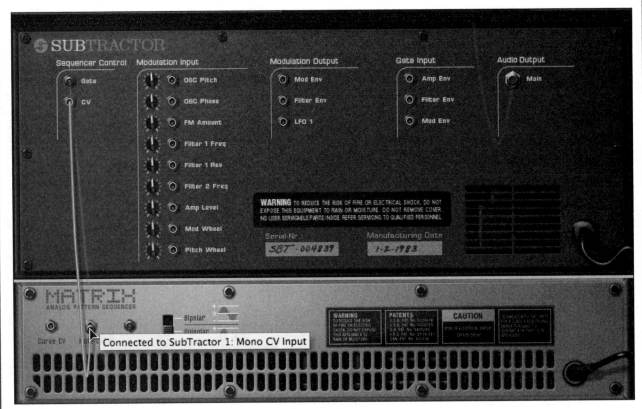

Figure 6.5 The Note CV to the CV input of the Subtractor.
Source: Propellerhead Software.

Gate CV Magic

It would almost seem unbelievable or counterintuitive, but having note data separate from the gate information can be quite cool. For example, you may run into a situation where you want to send gate information to the Amp Level (Volume control) to a fader on the mixer. This could, in turn, cause rhythmic gating. Having note data separate could be used in this example. You split the Note CV output coming from the Matrix going to several other CV inputs on several other synthesizers. This causes them all to play the same note. You could make it even crazier now by having gate information coming from several other Matrix sequencers, causing different devices to play in different rhythms.

With Control Voltages, or CV, it's important to note that you can seriously think outside of the Reason boxes. Examples like the one I mentioned can open up inspiration through simple cables and synthesizers that you wouldn't normally be entertained with through standard workflows. Keep following this exercise to get a better glimpse as to how this works!

4. Drag a patch cord from the Curve CV on the Matrix to the Filter 1 Freq (Frequency) and then turn the knob next to the input all the way up (see Figures 6.6 and 6.7). These small knobs control the strength of the modulation coming into the input. If the knob setting is low, the strength of the modulation is slight and not as apparent. When the knob setting is higher, the modulation is highly apparent. Press the Tab button when you finish.

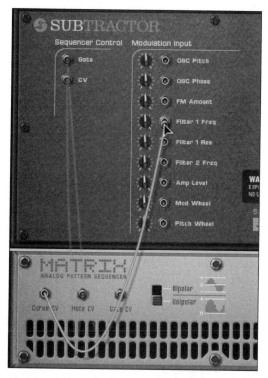

Figure 6.6 The Curve CV of the Matrix to the Filter 1 Freq Input on the Subtractor. Also shown are the Modulation Input knobs of the Subtractor.
Source: Propellerhead Software.

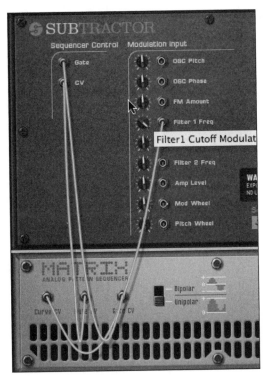

Figure 6.7 The Curve of the Matrix connected to the Filter 1 Freq.
Source: Propellerhead Software.

5. Programming a Matrix is simple and very similar to programming drum patterns, as we did in Chapter 3, "Arrangement and Composition Tricks." The main way to achieve success in understanding the Matrix is in the way that you look at it. Note information corresponds with the keyboard, which frames the right side of the Matrix program interface. If you turn the Matrix 90 degrees clockwise, you'll see that the graph next to the small keyboard (now below) directly affects the notes that are played in a Matrix sequence (see Figure 6.8). Try drawing some in!

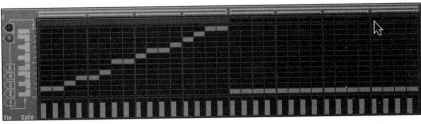

Figure 6.8 The Matrix on its side. Notice the way the notes work with the keyboard.
Source: Propellerhead Software.

6. The hash marks along the bottom of the Matrix display represent gate information (how long the note is held) and Velocity (how hard the note is played), as shown in Figure 6.9. You can use the Tie button to make the notes hold longer. The length depends on the Resolution knob setting. For example, if your resolution setting is set for a 16th note Matrix sequence, using the Tie setting on a Velocity hash would cause an 8th note to play within a 16th note sequence. One small trick is to hold down the Shift button while adjusting gate

information. Any Gate hash you touch while the Shift button is held will automatically tie. Try playing with the gate section now and pressing Shift periodically.

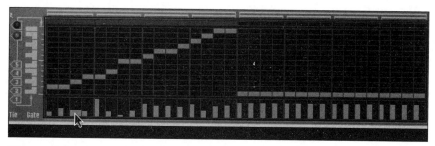

Figure 6.9 Adjust Gate and Velocity settings in the Matrix.
Source: Propellerhead Software.

7. When you have a Matrix pattern you really like, you'll find yourself wanting to hold on to it. This is easy, simply press the next Pattern button (see Figure 6.10). For example, if you're currently working on Pattern 1 (by default) on the Matrix, press the Pattern 2 button, and you'll have a brand new, empty pattern. There's no need to save. The Matrix holds on to each pattern until you save the song. Go ahead and fill Patterns 1–8 on the Matrix.

Figure 6.10 Use the Pattern buttons to move from pattern to pattern.
Source: Propellerhead Software.

Random and Alter Patch

Sometimes, it's fun to let Reason surprise you with a random melody, or even a slight alteration of your programmed melody. Try key commands like these*:

▶ **Randomize Pattern** (Cmd+R): Randomly generates a Matrix pattern.
▶ **Alter Pattern** (Shift+Cmd+P): Does a slight modification of your selected pattern.
▶ **Shift Pattern Down** (Shift+Cmd+D): Transposes the entire pattern down one step.
▶ **Shift Pattern Up** (Shift+Cmd+U): Transposes the entire pattern up one step.
▶ **Shift Pattern Left** (Cmd+J): Moves the pattern over one step.
▶ **Shift Pattern Right** (Cmd+K): Shifts pattern right one step.

*For PC, substitute Ctrl for Cmd.

Try out these suggested key commands, and you'll be generating patterns for the Matrix within seconds. If key commands aren't your thing, you can also right-click on the Matrix. The contextual menu features all of these same commands! Finally, if you want to get some great lead or bass lines, try turning the polyphony of the Subtractor down to 1.

8. Now, with your patterns filled, let me show you another aspect of the Matrix that you'll want to program as well. You'll notice a switch on the Matrix, near the keyboard graphic. It's labeled with Keys and Curve. Move the switch to the Curve position. While in Curve mode, you are able to draw in modulation patterns, instead of note patterns. If you remember, we routed the Curve modulation output to the Filter 1 Cutoff of the Subtractor. The Curve will be invisibly moving this knob up with the patterns that you create while in this mode. Note: The Curve patterns exist with each pattern you've already created. Add Curve modulation to Patterns 1–8 (see Figure 6.11). If you choose to use Randomize Pattern, listed in the previous tip section, you can skip this step, unless you want to modify the Curve pattern to something more specific. Randomize Pattern actually randomly generates Curve data as well.

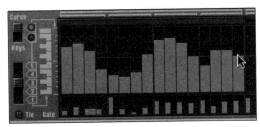

Figure 6.11 Add Curve modulation to Patterns 1–8.
Source: Propellerhead Software.

Cutoff Modulation

If you want to really hear more of an effect from your Curve patterns, try turning the Filter 1 Frequency knob down to about midway or lower. You can also adjust the way that the Matrix moves the Filter Frequency with the Bipolar/Unipolar switch on the back of the Matrix (see Figure 6.12). When in this mode, the Curve modulation goes two ways instead of one way. Example: The filter freq can be modulated in two directions with Bipolar, instead of always moving from one direction in Unipolar. The best way to understand it is to try it!

Figure 6.12 The Bipolar/Unipolar switch on the back of the Matrix.
Source: Propellerhead Software.

9. Okay, we have pattern data galore. It's time to make use of the Combinator encasing. Press the Show Programmer button on the Combinator. This will open up the command center for the Combinator and give you access to the power within (see Figure 6.13).

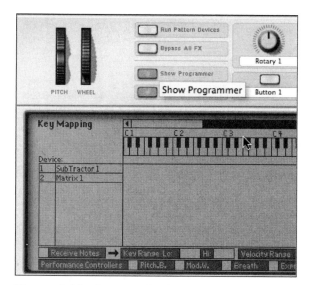

Figure 6.13 Open up the Combinator.
Source: Propellerhead Software.

10. Our next step is to assign some functionality to the knobs that adorn the front faceplate of the Combinator. These are important to know about within Reason because you can create some functionality within your Combinator patch that you would have never thought possible. For example, you can assign Knob 1 to control not only Filter 1 resonance, but also FM Modulation and Oscillator 2 detune, all with one knob twist. Think about the effect this would have! Go ahead and select Matrix 1 within the programmer, which will give you access to the parameter lists for the Matrix within the Modulation Routing table on the right (see Figure 6.14).

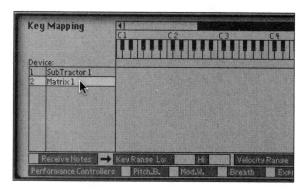

Figure 6.14 The Matrix selected in the Combinator programmer.
Source: Propellerhead Software.

11. With the Matrix selected in the programmer, assign Rotary 1 to the destination of Pattern Select using the Modulation Routing table (see Figure 6.15). This setting allows Rotary 1 to change different pattern numbers. The only problem is that you only have the first eight patterns available in the Matrix. If you turn the knob too far, empty patterns will start playing…this won't work.

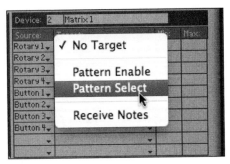

Figure 6.15 Select Pattern Select as your destination for Rotary 1.
Source: Propellerhead Software.

12. To fix the Rotary 1 issue with the Pattern Selection function, set the Min to 0 and the Max to 7. This fine-tunes the Combinator Rotary 1 functionality so that the lowest pattern selected by the knob is Pattern 1 and the highest pattern is Pattern 8 (see Figure 6.16).

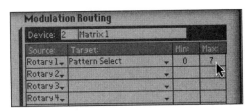

Figure 6.16 Fine-tune the Rotary 1 destination.
Source: Propellerhead Software.

13. Now that Rotary 1 is entirely functional, give it the name of Pattern Select, under the actual Rotary 1 knob (see Figure 6.17). Just click where it says Rotary 1, and it will turn blue; then type. It's important to get into the habit of labeling when creating Combinator patches, because it's easy to lose track of "what does what" really quickly, considering the infinite amount of devices you can add.

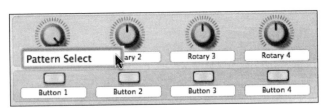

Figure 6.17 Label Rotary 1—Pattern Select.
Source: Propellerhead Software.

14. Next, in the Combinator programmer, select Subtractor 1, which will give you access to its parameter list within the Modulation Routing table. Assign Rotary 2 to Filter 1 Freq (see Figure 6.18). You'll remember that we assigned the Matrix Curve directly to the Subtractor Filter Freq earlier. This is okay, and will actually make this simple Combinator patch very fun. The Curve modulates the filter frequency, and you still have access to

choose the point where the modulation will start. It sounds a lot more interesting than actually reading it. Give it a whirl! Once you've made the assignment, label Rotary 2—Filter Freq (not shown).

Figure 6.18 Assigning Rotary 2 to Filter Freq of the Subtractor.
Source: Propellerhead Software.

You have now made a very simple performance-based Combinator, filled with sequences of your choice. At this point, I would highly advise saving your Reason session, as we will be adding to this Combinator in the next exercise. After all, this is very, very simple right now. We want to make it bigger, fuller, and more useable!

Hopefully, this Combinator begins to give you ideas for patches of your own, and also ways you can use Control Voltages to spice up even your regular Reason rack. The Control Voltages will always work the same, either in, or out, of the Combinator. Either way, consider using performance-based Combinators on stage or in the studio. By filling up a Matrix with fresh bass lines, leads, and so on, you will always have coolness to throw into your future tracks.

In the next exercise, we're going to start adding effects and other tricks for making this performance Combinator much more fun.

Effects Within a Combinator

You may have noticed that by having instruments working together within a Combinator, it's almost like you're creating a second studio environment. If you choose this to be true, then we are missing something vital: effects!

In this exercise, I'd like to show you a few Reason effects that greatly add dimension and width to Combinators, or as an insert, or send. For this exercise, you'll want to bring up the last Reason session with the Combinator we were building earlier. We're going to need it!

1. Right-click on the Subtractor in your Combinator and add an Echo device (see Figure 6.19). This is an amazing digital delay that can be used in many different ways. For this Combinator, we won't actually be using it for a delay. We'll be exploiting a secondary feature of the device.

Figure 6.19 Create an Echo.
Source: Propellerhead Software.

The Echo

If you have need of a really beautiful and versatile delay unit, look no further than the Echo. It's built with the classic sensibilities of some of the delay units built in the 1970s and 1980s, but has a few tricks that make it very modern, too. Its built-in modulation capabilities within the Modulation section of the Echo contain parameters like Wobble and Env (Envelope) that add subtlety to heavy detuning. The Echo even has an LFO of its own that you can use to modulate the overall pitch of the echoes coming out of this unit in harsh or subtle ways. The Color section is amazing for making those delayed parts fit within any song. Use the built-in optional filter to do this, and use the Drive to give it more character. We'll be using one of the side benefits of this unit in this exercise that goes beyond regular delay.

2. Switch the Echo's mode to Roll (see Figure 6.20). This mode corresponds with the Roll bar at the bottom of the unit. After this assignment is made, try playing with it. The best way to use it is to immediately push the bar to the right. It creates some crazy stutters! Try adjusting the Time knob, too, and then push the Roll bar again.

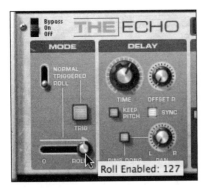

Figure 6.20 The Echo in Roll mode with the Roll bar.
Source: Propellerhead Software.

3. Click on the Echo within the Combinator programmer. Then assign Roll Enabled to Button 3, as shown in Figure 6.21. This parameter will move the Roll bar forward. The cool thing is that you'll have access to the Roll bar from the front of the Combinator along with the Subtractor and Matrix functions that we've chosen to centralize there. Label Button 3 as Stutter.

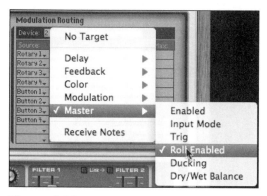

Figure 6.21 Assigning Button 3 to Roll Enabled in the Combinator.
Source: Propellerhead Software.

4. While you still have the Echo selected in the Combinator programmer, assign Knob 3 to Delay Time (see Figure 6.22). This will be a lot of fun, in the sense that you can choose stutter speeds and create pitch shifts. Also, you'll have the Delay Time and Roll functions side-by-side and easily accessible on a MIDI Controller, should you choose to use one. Label Knob 3 as Stutter Speed.

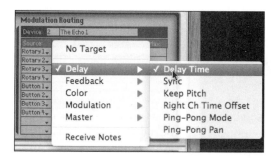

Figure 6.22 Assigning the Delay Time to Knob 3.
Source: Propellerhead Software.

Pitch Bending with the Echo

When you are using the Roll bar on the Echo and you adjust the timing, you'll notice that the pitch of what you are stuttering will bend. This effect can actually be turned off by pressing the Keep Pitch button on the Echo itself. However, before you elect to go with Keep Pitch all the time, remember, you can use this bending feature to simulate record scratches, create new effects, and more.

5. To further add to the coolness that you can have with clever use of Control Voltages, let's add something that will really make this stutter setup with the Echo a little different. Press the Tab button and locate the LFO 1 Modulation Output on the Subtractor (see Figure 6.23). Drag a patch cable to the Rotary 3 Modulation Input on the Combinator. We're going to add a little diversity to our stutters.

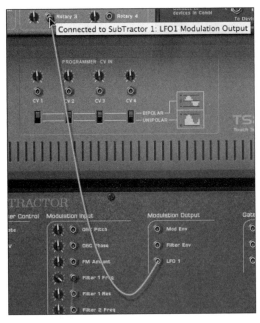

Figure 6.23 Drag a patch cable to the Rotary 3 input from the LFO 1 Modulation output.
Source: Propellerhead Software.

Low Frequency Oscillators

I use low frequency oscillators (LFO) to modulate parameters with waveforms of my choosing because they add texture and randomization to otherwise very cut-and-dry effects. If you ever find yourself wanting to have a knob or slider move up and down in a fixed pattern, try assigning LFO modulation to its Control Voltage input in the back of the Reason rack. Almost everything in Reason has a Control Voltage.

6. By setting up this routing, we can now modulate one of the Combinator's own functions with a Control Voltage coming from within it, that being the Subtractor. Remember, Rotary 3 is our Stutter Speed knob. By adding LFO modulation (low frequency oscillator), we're going to take our stutters to another level altogether. We're adding in randomization. On the front of the Subtractor, turn on Sync in the LFO 1 section (see Figure 6.24). Then set the waveform pattern to Random square wave. This will rhythmically change the Delay Time setting on the Echo, but it will occur during the stutter that we set up. Also, because the LFO will be random, you'll never really know when and what the stutter will sound like.

Figure 6.24 The LFO section of the Subtractor.
Source: Propellerhead Software.

7. Even though the LFO modulation of our stutter function will be random, it would be nice to know how random it will be. Let's assign a knob to the LFO 1 Rate, so that we give ourselves a little control. Click on the Subtractor in the Combinator programmer. Then set Rotary 4's destination to LFO 1 Rate, as shown in Figure 6.25. Label the knob LFO 1 Rate on the front of the Combinator. Or choose something more fitting like Randomization Rate. Once this is completed, spend some time playing with this by enabling the stutter and playing with the Stutter Speed knob and the LFO 1 Rate knob. It can get pretty wild.

Figure 6.25 Routing Rotary 4 to LFO 1 Rate.
Source: Propellerhead Software.

8. If you read the tip section on pitch bending, you'll know that having the Keep Pitch button on has a large effect on the sound of the Delay Time, in regard to the Echo. As the Keep Pitch function does drastically alter the behavior of our stutters, let's go ahead and assign a button on the Combinator to enable and disable this function. Click on the Echo in the Combinator programmer and then assign the Keep Pitch button to Button 4. This will make the stutters more rhythmic when we want, but with a touch of the button, we can have the crazy pitching come back. Make sure you label Button 4 as Keep Pitch (see Figure 6.26).

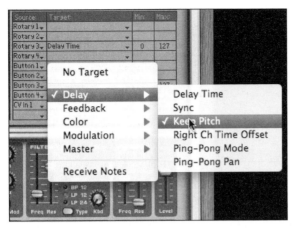

Figure 6.26 Assigning the Keep Pitch option to Button 4.
Source: Propellerhead Software.

9. Now it's time to add a little more depth to the synth sound we've been working with this whole time. If you've been following these exercises as-is, you've been working with a single sawtooth Subtractor patch. This isn't bad for light basses and leads, but if we want more bite, we need to put in some work. One thing that gives everything bite is the Pulveriser, which is found in the same Creative Effects section of the contextual menu as the Echo. Go ahead and right-click on the Echo and create a Pulveriser (see Figure 6.27). This will force the Echo through the Pulveriser. This means that the stutters will be pulverized, too. Once created, turn the Squash knob of the Pulveriser to 11 o'clock, and the Dirt knob to 12.

Figure 6.27 The Pulveriser and the Echo.
Source: Propellerhead Software.

10. Now, let's add an effect within an effect. Through Control Voltage routing, we're going to set up a phaser effect using some of the Pulveriser's other functions. On the back of the Pulveriser, send the Tremor Modulation output to the CV 1 input of the Combinator (see Figure 6.28). This is a generic CV on the Combinator

that can be assigned in any way we choose. Turn the strength of the CV 1 input on the Combinator to 9 o'clock. Because we're making a phaser, we don't want the effect to be too overt. We'll keep it a little subtle.

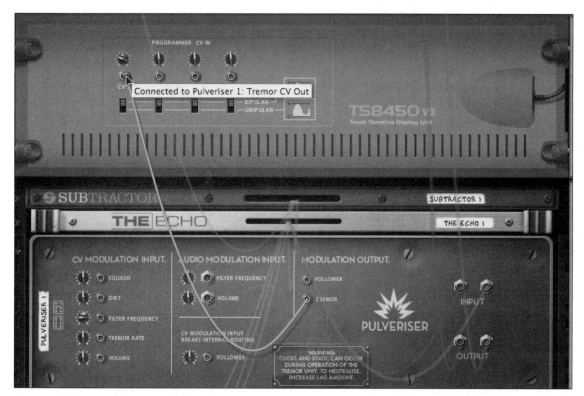

Figure 6.28 Routing the Tremor Output of the Pulveriser to the Combinator CV1 input.
Source: Propellerhead Software.

The Pulveriser

There are many different forms of compressors out there. In fact, Reason, itself, has two different types. You could also consider the Pulveriser a third, but it does more than compression. It's a distortion unit, compressor, and just an oddity beyond that. If you like compression, you will love the Pulveriser, as it makes the whole process fun and easy. The more compression you want, the more you raise the Squash knob. The more distortion you want, the more you raise the Dirt knob. If you need that sick, pulsing compression fast, lower the Release knob and raise the Squash to taste. It really is a great device.

Another really enjoyable function of the Pulveriser is the Tremor and Follower portion of the device. You can use the Tremor to modulate other portions of the Pulveriser, like the built-in filter. The Follower, which looks like the threshold of the compressor, actually is an assignable threshold that you can use to modulate the filter based on the incoming signal or the Tremor. And you can use it to modulate external devices from the Follower Control Voltage output. This is just another example of how every device in Reason can be used for something else. We'll be investigating the Pulveriser more as we continue through the book, along with many other effects devices.

11. In the Combinator programmer, select the Pulveriser as a device. In the Modulation Routing table, route Button 1 to Filter Mode (see Figure 6.29). We'll use this to enable and disable the Phaser function we are about to make. The default Min and Max actually work perfectly here. Select the empty Source slot down at the bottom of the Modulation Routing table and select CV in 1. This is the Control Voltage on the back that we cabled to from the Tremor modulation output on the back of the Pulveriser. Set the CV in 1 target to Filter Frequency. The Min should be 13, and the Max should be 90. Label Button 1 Phaser Bypass.

Modulation Routing				
Device: 3	Pulveriser 1			
Source:	Target:		Min:	Max:
Rotary 1 ▾		▾		
Rotary 2 ▾		▾		
Rotary 3 ▾		▾		
Rotary 4 ▾		▾		
Button 1 ▾	Filter Mode	▾	0	5
Button 2 ▾		▾		
Button 3 ▾		▾		
Button 4 ▾		▾		
CV In 1 ▾	Filter Frequency	▾	13	90
		▾		

Figure 6.29 The Modulation Routing of the Pulveriser.
Source: Propellerhead Software.

12. On the Pulveriser, set the Tremor Rate knob to 0 with Sync off. We're going for subtle, and slower is better for subtle. If you want to increase it later...wait. There is a plan for that. Trust me! Turn the Peak knob up to 12 o'clock (see Figure 6.30). Now, try pressing play in Reason, or pressing Run Pattern Devices on the Combinator. Listen to what you've done so far.

Figure 6.30 The filter section of the Pulveriser. Peak at 12 o'clock.
Source: Propellerhead Software.

13. Now for some finishing touches to put things right over the edge. Our wimpy sawtooth being supplied by the Subtractor sounds better through the Pulveriser, but it could use a little more "oomph." Let's spice things up. Select the Subtractor in the Combinator programmer (see Figure 6.31). Assign Button 2 to Osc2 On/Off. The Subtractor actually has two oscillators, and we're going to use one, as an option, to thicken up our synth in big bad ways. Label Button 2 as Thicker, or something along those lines. Get creative, if you like.

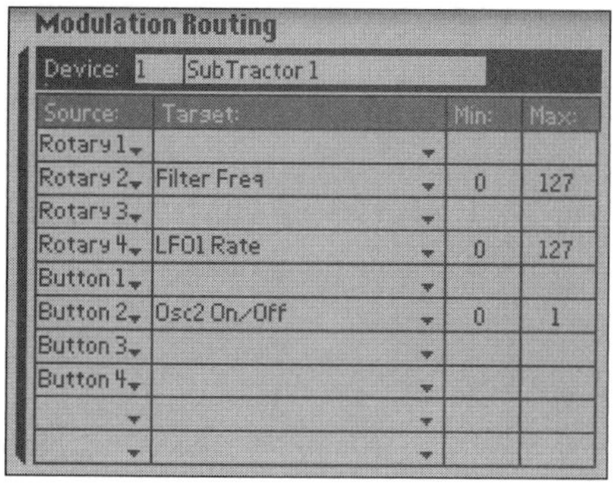

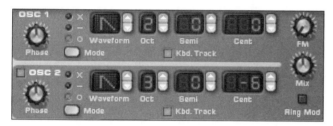

Figure 6.31 The Modulation Routing for the Subtractor.
Source: Propellerhead Software.

14. On the Subtractor, we need to make some changes to Oscillator 2, so that it's a little more evil than the first. Based on my Matrix patterns, I actually set OSC 2 so that it is one octave higher than the first oscillator (see Figure 6.32). I have OSC 1 at an Octave setting of 2, and Osc 2 at an octave of 3. I took OSC 2 down to -6 on the Cents setting so that it is slightly detuned from Oscillator 1.

Figure 6.32 My Subtractor Oscillator settings.
Source: Propellerhead Software.

Thickening Synths

If you're ever working with a Subtractor and decide that you would like to thicken up the sound of the patch you are working with, you have a couple of options here. The first option is to add a second oscillator and detune it from the first oscillator, as we did in the last step of this exercise. Subtle to harsh detunings have been thickening up synthesizers of all sorts for years. You can also modify the Phase Mode of the oscillators on the Subtractor. See Figure 6.33 for a glimpse of the Phase Mode settings. Try putting the Phase in either "-" or "x" and then assign LFO 2, or 1, to Phase. Once the Phase is modulating, you will get a much thicker sound.

Figure 6.33 The Subtractor Oscillator Phase sections.
Source: Propellerhead Software.

15. Let's come up with a way to control the rate of the phaser from the Combinator faceplate. We've used all the knobs and buttons, so we'll need to get creative. Why not the Mod Wheel? Select Pulveriser in the Combinator programmer and set up the Mod Wheel as a source in the Modulation Routing table. Set the Mod. W. target to Tremor Rate (see Figure 6.34). Give it a Min of 0 and a Max of 40. When you turn the Mod Wheel now, you'll be able to control the modulation rate of the Pulveriser Tremor, which is controlling the Comb Filter. Raising the Mod Wheel will greatly increase the thickness of the synth and have it stand out more. You can use this when you have a lot of space in your song.

Modulation Routing

Device: 3 Pulveriser 1

Source:	Target:	Min:	Max:
Rotary 1			
Rotary 2			
Rotary 3			
Rotary 4			
Button 1	Filter Mode	0	5
Button 2			
Button 3			
Button 4			
CV In 1	Filter Frequency	13	90
Mod.W	Tremor Rate	0	40

Figure 6.34 The Modulation Routing Table for the Pulveriser with the Mod W/Tremor Rate settings.
Source: Propellerhead Software.

16. Working with this Combinator, you may decide that you'd rather play the synth than have the Matrix do it. After all, we do have a nice thick synth tone now. The only thing is, we don't want the Mod Wheel settings of the Subtractor to interfere with the Phaser Mod Wheel trick we set up. Let's fix this. Click on the Subtractor in the Combinator programmer. Under the Key Mapping section of the Combinator programmer, uncheck the Mod. W. check box at the bottom of the Key Mapping Section (see Figure 6.35). Unchecking this box will turn off the Combinator's ability to trigger the Mod Wheel of the Subtractor.

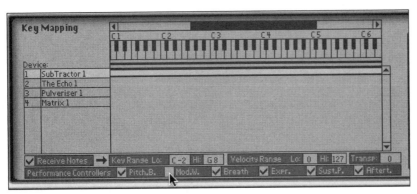

Figure 6.35 Disabling Mod Wheel functionality for the Subtractor within the Combinator Programmer.
Source: Propellerhead Software.

Combinator Key Mapping Check Boxes

By Default, any instrument that you throw into a Combinator will be trigger-able by your MIDI controller. And this is great, unless you don't want to trigger certain devices within your Combinator. For example, you have a Malstrom synthesizer that you are only using for the filters, not for its tone-making abilities. Or you're doing a performance-based Combinator that doesn't need MIDI functionality because everything is trigger-able from the Combinator faceplate. Should this need arrive, disable Receive notes at the bottom of the Key Mapping section of the Combinator programmer. It's a small check box right at the bottom. You'll also notice other check boxes for Sustain Pedal, after Touch, Breath, and more. You can actually make it where one device in the programmer has, for example, Mod Wheel trigger-ability, where another one doesn't. It's just another way that Propellerhead has made it where you can truly make instruments that you've always wanted through the Combinator.

17. I would highly encourage you to try playing the keyboard, too, and experimenting with the Matrix sequencer being active. To disable the sequencer, simply press Run Pattern Devices or stop the sequencer. This patch is very fun to play with when the Matrix is off, too, while still using the stutter function we set up. See Figure 6.36 for the Run Pattern Devices button.

Figure 6.36 The Run Pattern Devices button.
Source: Propellerhead Software.

18. We're done! The only thing left is to save this patch. Press the Save button on the top section of the Combinator (see Figure 6.37). From here, you can choose where you want to save your patch, what the name will be, and so on. This will also make the patch available to other songs you are working on in the future.

Figure 6.37 Save the patch by pressing the Save button.
Source: Propellerhead Software.

Conclusion

Hopefully, you've picked up on the coolness of Control Voltages and Combinators at this point. They both add such a versatility to your patch making that is almost unbelievable when you think about it.

This particular patch we've been creating is a hybrid of being a pattern-based Combinator and an instrument patch. Just one of the many types that we'll be exploring!

In the next chapter, we're going to get into Combinator Effects patches. This is where the Combinator is only being used as an effects device, holding several effects devices. We'll also start looking at Performance Combinators, which will allow you to be a one-man, or a one-woman band.

See you in the next chapter!

Effects Combinators

7

EFFECTS ARE A MAJOR PART OF MUSIC. They create dimension, atmosphere, and style within any song you throw them into. Reason has tons of different FX devices within its library of devices, and they all work very similarly to their hardware counterparts. But you may be missing a device that works specifically to your specific taste. For example, you may want a reverb device that also has built-in chorus. Or you may want a compressor with some extra EQ settings and so on.

Thankfully, the Combinator does more than just combine instruments to form new instruments. You can also use the Combinator as an FX device. Imagine being able to combine several of your favorite Reason effects combinations into one device, and then have that particular combination of effects already there for you in one streamlined patch that's to your liking.

If you think about it, through the act of combining several effects modules, mixing devices, and so on, it really is like you're building a new device altogether. For example, even when hardware manufacturers design an effects device from scratch, they aren't actually designing every piece of hardware that goes into the device. They are buying multiple circuit boards, capacitors, meters, and in some cases, modules from other manufacturers that they put into their own device. Once the act of planting each device into the chassis of the new unit is complete and the initial soldering has been finished, a whole new set of tasks come in where the engineer has to get each knob and button actually working through wiring. This generally involves more soldering, experimenting, and so on.

What you're doing inside of a Combinator is exactly the same! The only difference is that this is all taking place in a contained environment where you can't set anything on fire, and there is no risk of burning yourself on a soldering iron.

Like the last chapter, we'll be building a very intricate Combinator device over the course of an exercise. With this in mind, be sure to save regularly. Once you've completed these exercises, you'll most likely have a long list of ideas of your own. This is great! Remember, you can always go back and backward-engineer together all the things we built within this book. You can always go into the Reason factory sound bank and backward-engineer anything you find in there as well.

This particular exercise is going to focus less on Control Voltages and more on ways where you can optimize your Combinator programming in terms of the following:

   ▷ Learning new ways to utilize rotaries
   ▷ Optimizing your usage of buttons
   ▷ Using the rotaries for more than just turning other knobs up and down (a few tricks)
   ▷ Uncovering hidden secrets of a few devices in Reason that you'll really want to know about

Okay, now that we have a clear understanding of what we'll be doing, let's move into the anatomy of Combinator for FX.

The Combinator for FX

If you look at the back of a Combinator, you'll notice that there are two inputs going to and from devices within the Combinator. These inputs and outputs are the gateway from the internal rack of the Combinator into the more expansive song rack of Reason. You also have two inputs and outputs directly above these internal inputs and outputs (see Figure 7.1).

Figure 7.1 The Combinator inputs and outputs.
Source: Propellerhead Software.

These inputs and outputs connect the mixer of Reason with the internal rack of the Combinator. So far, we've only really used the Combinator output. When the Input is utilized as well, Reason will consider this new device as an effect and treat it differently, which you will see over the course of this chapter.

More Reason Mixers

Because there are a limited number of inputs and outputs, it is sometimes necessary to use a mixer within a Combinator, even if it's an effect. This guarantees that multiple signals will all make their way to the final output of the Combinator.

Reason actually does have a few different mixers in addition to the main mixer discussed in Chapter 2, "Song Creation Workflows in Reason." These are actually legacy devices from back when Reason didn't have a main mixer. But, believe me, they are still highly useful, in the sense that they allow you to blend signals within Combinators.

Mix and Audio Channels

Mix Channel devices and Audio Track devices are essentially Combinators that have been specifically designed to carry out a more specified role, that of routing audio through to the mixer. Deep in the core of both of these devices, however, beats the heart of a fierce Combinator. Included in both of these devices are programmers that are very similar to a Combinator's programmer, an internal rack section that can hold additional effects, instruments, and assignable CV inputs and rotaries.

I mention this to you because if you know how to program a Combinator, you also understand how to program Mix and Audio Track devices. There's no difference, aside from minor cosmetics. The only big difference will be the Dynamics input for sidechaining.

Basic Effects Combinator

This exercise will teach you how to create a very basic effects Combinator, and then instruct you in ways that you can set up specific knob values to give you cool effects without causing distortion and feedback.

Keep in mind, it's okay to experiment with different values as you move from step to step. But, once you've experimented, you will definitely want to move the values over to the specified values within the exercise, so that you can also hear why I'm suggesting such values. There's always a reason!

To start this exercise, we will be setting up a Dr. Octo Rex as a signal source. It's a big deal to be able to hear what's going through your effects patch, right?

1. Create a Dr. Octo Rex, as shown in Figure 7.2. This is an ideal instrument for what we're doing, as it actually does play back recordings of real instruments. Also, the recordings can be played back at any speed.

Figure 7.2 The Dr. Octo Rex.
Source: Propellerhead Software.

2. Press the Browse Patch button (see Figure 7.3). It's possible to load up several different loops into one Dr. Octo Rex or to load up a single loop. In this case, we'll be loading up a full patch with several loops contained within.

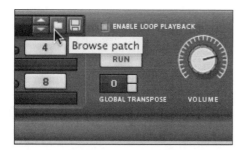

Figure 7.3 The Browse Patch button.
Source: Propellerhead Software.

3. In the Reason Factory Sound Bank, locate Dr. Octo Rex Patches → Guitar Loops → Electric Rhythm Guitar → Cherie Rhythm 105 → Major Scales → El Guitar | Cherie Key of A 105 BPM. After you've loaded up the patch,

try pressing the Run button or your spacebar (see Figure 7.4). Press Buttons 1 through 8 and notice the different chords being played in the same rhythm. You can run a guitar loop periodically to hear the work that you're doing as you make your effects Combinator.

Figure 7.4 The Dr. Octo Rex loaded with a guitar patch.
Source: Propellerhead Software.

Dr. Octo Rex and Instrument Loops

Believe it, or not, you can use the Dr. Octo Rex patches like the one used in this exercise to add guitars easily into your songs, even if you don't know how to play. All of the Dr. Octo Rex guitar patches are made up of several different guitar chords being strummed in a rhythm that will be identical or similar. Because you have several guitar loops to switch between that all keep the same timing, you can actually record your loop changes in a song. When this occurs, it makes it almost impossible to tell later that you didn't use a guitarist. In fact, technically, you did use a guitarist because you actually are playing back loops of a real guitarist. Try it out!

---

4. Create a Scream Sound Destruction unit and an RV7000 Advanced Reverb (see Figure 7.5). These devices will be at the core of your simple FX Combinator. They are also an extremely cool pairing with an electric guitar. You get your thick distortion device that will be reverberated, or delayed, by the programmable reverb/delay. There are really a lot of possibilities here!

Figure 7.5 The Scream Distortion unit and the RV7000 Reverb.
Source: Propellerhead Software.

The Order

When using multiple effects devices, the order in which you patch one device through another can have a great impact on how things actually sound. Take our current setup with the Scream going into a reverb. If I were to play it right now, it would sound like a distorted guitar going through a reverb. However, if I reversed the signal path, where the reverb went through the distortion unit, it would sound like a reverberating guitar being severely distorted. The sound is actually quite different. I'd highly encourage you to toy with signal flow.

5. Shift-select both the Scream and the RV7000 (see Figure 7.6). Do not include the Dr. Octo Rex in this selection. When you have the blue field around both devices, right-click and select Combine. This will, of course, add the devices into a new Combinator.

Figure 7.6 Two effects devices combined.
Source: Propellerhead Software.

Device Description: About Scream and RV7000

The Scream Sound Destruction Unit and the RV7000 Reverb unit share a special place in Reason history. Both units were released in the Reason 2.5 update that was a free update for licensed, registered Reason users. Both devices were highly complementary in the sense that one gives you a hellish, raw sound, and the other adds ambience and an ethereal quality to everything else.

The Scream, in particular, gives you several settings of distortion. Each distortion setting is highly unique, in the sense that changing to a different distortion setting will also greatly change the character of whatever source signal you run through the device.

With every distortion setting, the P1 and P2 knobs will change to a different function that will grant distortion modifiers that are applicable for the type of distortion that you're using. For example, switching to the Digital Setting on Scream will change the P1 and P2 knobs over to Resolution and Rate, like Sample Resolution and Sample Rate.

When dialing through the different distortions, or Damage Types, available within the Scream devices, don't forget to adjust the P1 and P2 modifiers. You may only actually find the Damage Type you like after you modify the parameters first.

Also included within the Scream unit, but not at all to be forgotten, are the Cut (EQ) and Body sections. Keep a special eye on the Body section. You can use this section to add Resonant body to your source signal, very similar to running your source signal through different speaker cabinet types.

Scream isn't the only distortion device within Reason, but it's definitely one of the more unique, and can be used to give you guitar, bass, synth, vocals, organ, or whatever else you can think of that creates a unique attitude that will not be easily forgotten.

The RV7000 is actually a very advanced Reverb unit. It houses several, highly useful reverb algorithms, an EQ, and a Gate. The EQ is great for dialing in that reverb (and only reverb) that needs to add spaciousness without mud. There are only two bands available for adjustment, but with the ability to add as many additional EQ units as you want, who's complaining?

Gate section is wonderful for creating gated reverbs in a way that is both in the box and outside of it. You can set up a threshold so that any signal that surpasses it will get reverb, and any that doesn't, won't. There is also the possibility of triggering via MIDI or Control Voltage as well.

But these modes are just the tip of the iceberg! The algorithms are where things get really interesting. There are algorithms that we all have come to love and appreciate like Hall, Auditorium, and Gate. But there are also some algorithms that are more esoteric like Reverse and Spring. Each algorithm has several settings that are unique and allow you to really create original effects that can add a completely new sound to your source signal.

6. Press the Tab button now. Notice how the routing from the Dr. Octo Rex is still intact. Try playing your loop device and notice how everything is still working. Reason is intelligent enough to know that when you chose to combine multiple effects devices, you wanted an effects Combinator. This caused Reason to auto-route into the Dr. Octo Rex and into the Combinator Input, thus setting the Combinator up as an effect, not an instrument (see Figure 7.7).

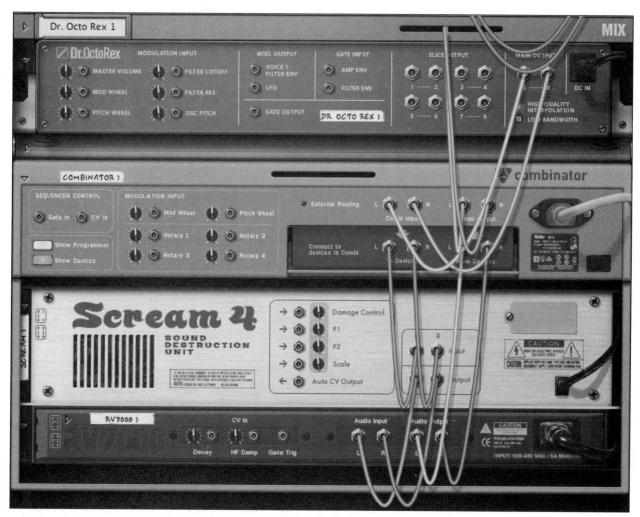

Figure 7.7 The cabling of the effects Combinator.
Source: Propellerhead Software.

7. If you play the Dr. Octo Rex, you'll notice that at this point, it sounds like a muddy mess. Let's get things into a state that is more conducive for our work. We'll start by setting up the Scream unit with some settings we enjoy. In order to hear it clearly, let's set up a Bypass button for the RV7000. Open the Combinator programmer and select the RV7000. Map Button 1 to Master → Enabled. Set the Min to 1 and the Max to 2. This will

cause Button 1, when pressed, to put the RV7000 into Bypass mode, and when depressed, to put the RV7000 into the On position (see Figure 7.8). Label this button: Delay Bypass.

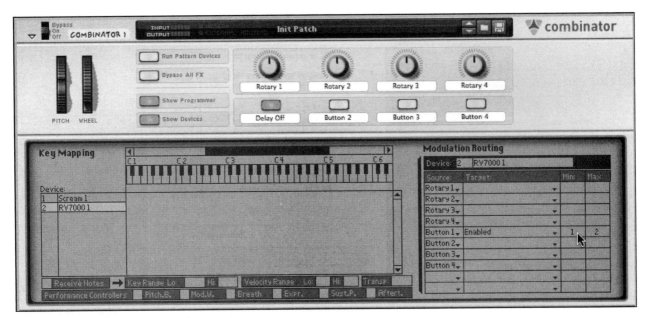

Figure 7.8 Programming the RV7000 Bypass button.
Source: Propellerhead Software.

8. With the RV7000 temporarily disabled with a new button, let's focus on the Scream unit. Set the Scream's Damage Type to Fuzz (see Figure 7.9). This will give the guitar loop a very gritty sound instantly.

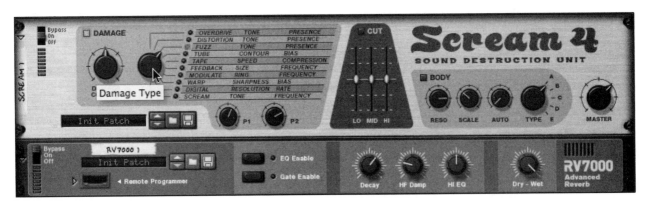

Figure 7.9 Setting the Damage Type on the Scream.
Source: Propellerhead Software.

9. Try adjusting the P1 and P2 knobs on the Scream unit now. In the Fuzz mode, these knobs are actually adjusting Tone and Presence, if you look next to the Fuzz setting in the Damage FX Table. Try adjusting both knobs and notice the difference that they make in the overall sound of the guitar. Let's assign both of the Scream

parameter knobs to one of the Combinator knobs. But we'll do a spin on it. Go ahead and assign these knobs now by going to the Combinator programmer and selecting the Scream unit within the Programmer. Assign Rotary 1 to Parameter 1 (Damage), and then on the next line, assign Rotary 1 to Parameter 2 (see Figure 7.10).

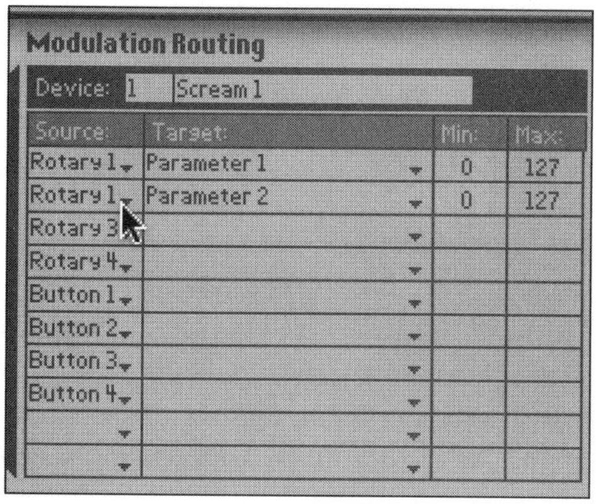

Figure 7.10 Assigning one Rotary to two parameters.
Source: Propellerhead Software.

10. Obviously, we don't want the Parameter knobs doing the same thing when we turn Rotary 1. This is where we get creative with the Min and Max settings (see Figure 7.11). I'd like to set up a bit of an in-between, customized sound of my own that I could morph between when I turn Rotary 1. When I was moving around the Parameter 1 and 2 knobs, I discovered two distinct settings that I really liked:

Parameter 1 & 2—26 & 89
Parameter 1 & 2—109 & 38

I'd like to set it up where, instead of having a distinct jump from one setting to another, I'd rather have a gradual transition, or a morph. Try this out: set your Parameter 1 Rotary assignment to a Min of 26 and a Max of 109. Then set your Parameter 2 assignment of Rotary 1 to 89 and 38. Once you've done this, try adjusting Rotary 1 and notice how the knobs are moving from defined positions but in varying degrees. This is great for fine-tuned, specialized settings. Label the knob Tone Morph when you're finished.

Figure 7.11 Customized Min and Max settings give interesting knob movements.
Source: Propellerhead Software.

Multi-Rotary

In the last step, we assigned multiple parameters on one device to one rotary knob. This allows for very intense reactions from our Combinator patch with the simple turn of a knob. This also allows for very exact sound formulae based on your own personal preference in tones, behaviors, and more. In the end, it's really like you're building your own piece of gear with your exact sound specifications. But let's take it a step farther. What if you assigned the parameters of several different devices within your Combinator to one Rotary? Imagine the sonic hell you could create!

11. As we're working with the guitar, now would be a wonderful time to create some easy filtering action to make our guitar blend in better, in certain situations. Or, just for effect, in certain parts of the song. The Scream unit has a wonderfully simple EQ built into it that would work great (see Figure 7.12). I've set mine up where the mid range is slightly boosted, and the high and low is slightly cut. Go ahead and make some EQ settings that sound right for you.

Figure 7.12 The Scream Cut/EQ section.
Source: Propellerhead Software.

12. Now, let's program a Combinator button to enable and disable the Cut section. In the Combinator programmer, with Scream selected, assign Button 2 EQ → Cut On/Off. This will allow you to enable what is essentially a Band Pass filter, due to the settings of the Cut section of Scream. We all use a little midrange, every now and then, to make a guitar fit a little better. Here, you have this setting at the press of a button. Label the Button 2 as Cut (see Figure 7.13).

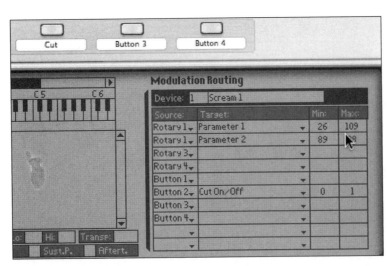

Figure 7.13 Programming a Combinator button to enable Cut.
Source: Propellerhead Software.

Choose Your Buttons Wisely

Sometimes you only need to enable one section of a device to get a particular sound. In the last step, we set up a specific section to be enabled by the Combinator. Because this section (Cut) was previously programmed with EQ settings, I only need to enable the Cut section to hear my work. Sometimes, it's nice to have a simple setting that you can bring in easily with a button press, rather than wasting several buttons and knobs to control one section of one device that lies within the Combinator.

13. Now it's time to start bringing the RV7000 into the action; go ahead and press the Delay/On button to hear it again. Once active, turn the Dry-Wet Knob to 12 o'clock so that you hear a part of the dry signal and part of the wet, or reverberated signal (see Figure 7.14).

Figure 7.14 Moving the Dry-Wet Knob on the RV7000.
Source: Propellerhead Software

14. Select the RV7000 in the Combinator programmer. We're going to utilize a very cool feature of the Combinator: its ability to map its buttons to features that aren't as easily accessed on other devices. Assign Button 3 to Master → Algorithm. By assigning a button to this parameter on the RV7000, you're allowing the Combinator to toggle two specific effect algorithms that reside within this massive reverb unit. What's great about this is that it's actually not that easy to change the RV7000 algorithms because the knob is smaller, and if the unit is condensed within the rack, you can't access it at all. Set the Min to 1 and the Max to 7. Through these numerical assignments, we're telling the Combinator to access the Room algorithm, when the Combinator button is unlit. When the button is lit, it's accessing the Multi tap delay setting on the RV7000. So, we're toggling from a nice, room-type effect to a massive, echo-type effect with the touch of a Button. Label Button 3 Room/Delay, as shown in Figure 7.15.

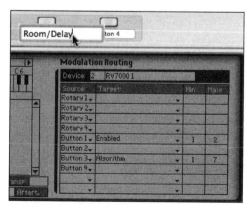

Figure 7.15 Setting up Button 3 on the RV7000.
Source: Propellerhead Software.

Multi Tap

By default, the Multi Tap algorithm on the RV7000 is actually set up as only a two-tap delay. It is capable of up to four, though! To access the third and fourth tap on this delay, you'll need to:

▶ Utilize the Multi Tap algorithm.
▶ Turn the Tap Level up for Taps 3 and 4.

Use the Edit Select knob in the RV7000 programmer when in the Multi Tap mode to toggle over to Taps 3 and 4. You'll notice that their Tap Levels are down all the way. Once you raise the Tap Level for either of these additional delays, you'll notice an extra line in the visual display for each additional tap. And, even better, when you play a signal through the RV7000, you'll have that much more echo.

15. With the toggle ability between two different algorithms, or reverb types, in this Combinator set up, I'd like to show you some extra functionality of the RV7000. Click on the Rotary 2 destination slot with the RV7000 selected within the Combinator programmer. Notice that the Room algorithm and the Multi Tap (actually condensed to Tap in this menu) algorithm are both listed as subdirectories. If you move into the Tap subdirectory, you'll notice that you have additional control over several smaller, but powerful, parameters of the RV7000. For example, you could control the delay time of Tap 1 if you mapped to Multi Tap 1 Delay (steps). Go ahead and do this now. Then map Rotary 3 to Multi Tap 2 Delay (steps). Label Rotary 2, Tap 1 and label Rotary 3, Tap 2. See Figure 7.16 for reference. Once you have this set up, try using the knobs. You might notice they don't work. This is because of some very quirky functionality within the RV7000. Move on to the next step to learn more.

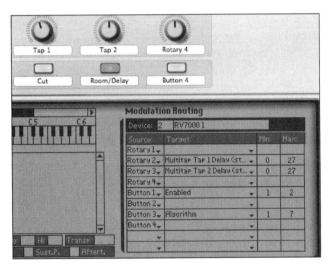

Figure 7.16 Multi Tap setup on the Combinator.
Source: Propellerhead Software.

16. In order for the knobs to work, you'll need to activate Tempo Sync on the RV7000 while it's in the Multi Tap algorithm. We've already set up the RV7000 to go there from the Combinator, so simply press the Room/Delay button so that it's lit up. Next, in the RV7000 programmer, turn the knob next to Tempo Sync. When you move the knobs now, while the signal is coming through your Combinator (Dr. Octo Rex), you'll be able to control the Tap times individually of the Multi Tap algorithm of the RV7000.

What's with the RV7000 Multi Tap?

This functionality has been long discussed with many a Combinator programmer. Why can you only map to synced delay taps in the Multi Tap mode of the RV7000? I can only speculate at the reasoning behind this. Most likely, it has something to do with the period in which the RV7000 was introduced to Reason, which was around Reason 2.5. The computers during this time weren't always fast enough to run Multi Tap delays without experiencing some major hiccups. In order to keep Reason functionality stable, they may have opted to keep the delays reigned in through the Tempo Sync barrier to ensure that no severe performance drop was introduced.

17. Finally, let's give some attention to the Room Algorithm that we have as an option within this Combinator. Press the Room/Delay button we set up, so that it's unlit. This will pop us back into the Room algorithm, which will also be apparent by the RV7000's display. Now, that we're in the Room Algorithm, the two knobs that we set up for the Multi Tap will not work. We can use this to our advantage, though! We can also map Room Algorithm functions to these knobs as well that will work entirely differently when we're in the Room mode of our Combinator. Of course, we'll need to relabel them, but this is a small price to pay, right? Let's map Room → Room Shape to Rotary 2, and Room → Room Size to Rotary 3. This will allow us to easily control the size and shape of our room from the Combinator front panel, and will in no way impede our Multi Tap settings. You'll also want to relabel Rotary 2 so that it says Room/Tap 1, and Rotary 3, so that it reads Size/Tap 2 (see Figure 7.17). This will be awesome, because now we have intuitive controls for both algorithms within the Combinator and the ability to bounce between two modes as well.

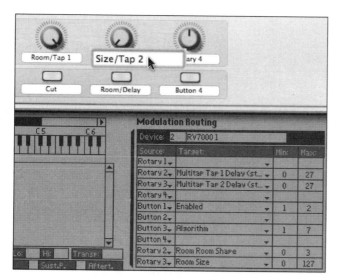

Figure 7.17 Knob sets with Room Algorithm added.
Source: Propellerhead Software.

Multiple Effect Toggles

As this last step has proved, you can have multiple knobs and buttons for multiple parameters within the RV7000 when using the Combinator. The only caveat is that you have to be in the algorithm of the parameter in question for this to work. For example, the rotary for Room Size only works when you are in the Room Size algorithm. This can be used to your advantage quite a bit, though. It would be very easy to set up a Combinator patch that toggles between several of the RV7000 algorithms with toggle buttons, and then has Rotaries controlling features that you use all the time, and no mapping to features that you don't use. Or, using our current Combinator as an example, a Combinator patch that has two reverb settings and a distortion setting all in there together. With the RV7000 and the Combinator, there's a lot of room for experimentation.

18. Now, it would be nice to set up a way to control the decay of the reverb, as well as the decay of the Multi Tap mode. Thankfully, the RV7000 Decay knob is global for all of the algorithms within the reverb unit. Map Rotary 4 to Master → Decay. Label Rotary 4 as Decay, as shown in Figure 7.18. We'll have a way to make the reverb and echoes much longer now. Granted, we're running guitar through this at the moment. But keep in mind that this effects device that we're creating can also be used for any other type of instrument or audio signal. It might as well be versatile.

Figure 7.18 Decay knob as it is added to the Combinator.
Source: Propellerhead Software.

19. One button left! What could we do with it? This would be a good time to add in a little EQ for the reverb. The RV7000 actually has a very cool EQ incorporated into itself. This feature is very helpful for getting mud out of your reverb or even adding some air to it. Of course, there are already Hi EQ and HF Damp (High Frequency damp) knobs on the RV7000. And I would highly encourage you to dial these in to get your reverb to a sound that you really like. In the meantime, let's get started on that EQ. Click the light next to the EQ label, down by the Edit Mode selector button. Yes, you can use the Edit Mode button, too. However, simply clicking the light will get you into this mode faster. Once you are inside, set the Low Gain to –9.3 and the Low Freq to 255 Hz. Set the Param Gain to 2.0 and the Freq to 5,124 Hz. The Q Param will be 0.2. This will reduce a lot of the mud caused by the reverb and add just a hint of air, over the top. Refer to Figure 7.19 for the settings as they appear in my RV7000.

Figure 7.19 The EQ section of the RV7000.
Source: Propellerhead Software.

20. In order for the EQ setting to be heard on the RV7000, you have to actually enable it. This is where we're actually going to utilize the Combinator. We'll use the Button 4 on the Combinator to be the On button. With the RV7000 selected, set Button 4's destination to Master → EQ On/Off. This will allow you to quickly initiate that cut/boost when you need it. Label Button 4 as Reverb EQ (see Figure 7.20).

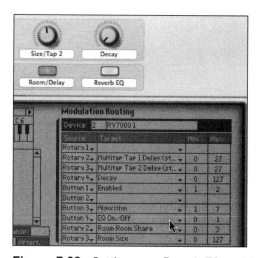

Figure 7.20 Setting up a Reverb EQ enable button.
Source: Propellerhead Software.

21. Okay, so things are essentially finished for this FX Combinator, and it's time to save (see Figure 7.21). Press the Save Patch button and save your new Combinator to a location where you can retrieve it easily. This is important for the next step of the exercise. I would highly recommend setting up a folder on your computer that houses not only your own personal patches for FX, but also for synthesizers, samples, and anything that you customize for Reason.

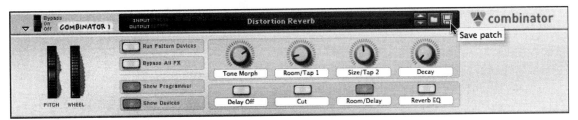

Figure 7.21 Save your Combinator Patch.
Source: Propellerhead Software.

Refills

Reason has a proprietary file format for its sounds and patches from both Propellerhead, third-party sound designers, sample libraries, and so on. This file format is known as a Refill. If you ever go onto www.propellerheads.se/downloads/refills, you'll discover an amazing library of...libraries! There are both free refills, as well as commercial refills, and they add so much to the Reason experience. What's even better is that there are more being added all the time.

Propellerhead has also made several commercial and free contributions of their own that are more than worth your attention. One Refill is the RB-338 Rebirth Refill. This refill contains all of the old samples from Rebirth, the program that Reason basically succeeded. You'll find wonderful 808 and 909 drum kits that will rock your world, as well as TB-303 sounds from the classic Roland synth. It's a lot of fun and can instantly add to any song you're working on. This is a free Refill, and the only requirement, like all the free refills I'm listing would be that you have to be a registered user.

There are also the major contributions of Kurt Kurasaki, a long-time friend, Reason guru, and fellow author who has several staple refills and Combinators at www.peff.com. You can also find countless articles that are highly intense, well written, and will definitely catapult you into areas of knowledge in Reason far beyond mere mortals. Kurt is one of the main guys traveling the world preaching the gospel of Reason. Trust me, this is good stuff. And, beyond making many of the sounds that have shipped with Reason, he's also one of the guys responsible for many of the default effects Combinators.

There are also the JB series refills from the Propellerhead Product Specialist, James Bernard. I've worked with James on several occasions when I was contributing to the factory sound banks for Reason, and he's amazing. If you're interested in learning how to take your sound design in Reason to the next level, I'd seriously recommend backward-engineering some of his patches. You'll have your mind blown.

There are several commercial Refills that I would recommend as well. The Reason Drum Kits 2.0 is an amazingly detailed multi-sampled set of drums. There are several MIDI files as well, if you don't like programming your own drumbeats, too. These are all so real, no one will know the difference.

Reason Pianos has several major pianos lovingly recorded, multi-sampled, and multi-layered. I've used Combinators from this refill several times, and when I've played back songs that feature these pianos, I've actually had people ask, "What piano did you use?"

Obviously, if you're reading this book, you own Reason. With that in mind, get out there and find some Refills that match your work style. You'll learn a lot from seeing how the patches are built, and you'll gain sounds that will catapult you forward into new levels of professionalism.

22. Now that you've saved, I'd like you to try a little experiment. Create a Mix Channel from the Create menu → Other submenu. Once you've created the Mix Channel, press the Show Programmer button. Within this programmer area, you'll notice some similarities to the Combinator front that you've been working in. There are four buttons and four knobs. It's all there. You'll also notice that there is a Browse Patch and Save Patch button as well (see Figure 7.22).

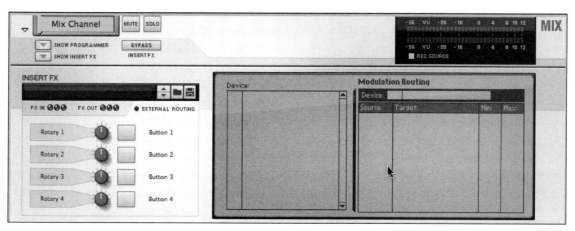

Figure 7.22 The Programmer screen of the Mix Channel device.
Source: Propellerhead Software.

23. Press the Browse Patch button. This will bring up the Reason Patch browser that you are, by now, very used to seeing. Browse to the new patch directory that you created for yourself that contains the simple effects Combinator that we created over this exercise. Once you've located it, notice that it's not grayed out or invisible. You can actually choose to open this patch within this other, similar device. In fact, why don't you try to open it? See Figure 7.23.

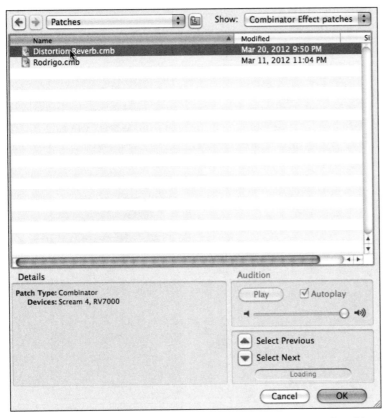

Figure 7.23 The Reason Patch Browser with the effects Combinator available.
Source: Propellerhead Software.

24. Once you've opened up the Combinator patch within the Mix Channel device, and you see that they are one and the same, you should be feeling like you are really empowered. This means that all that routing work you've been doing in a Combinator can be reused in Mix Channels and audio tracks within Reason. In fact, what this fully reveals is that FX Combinators can be used as inserts within your songs.

25. Need a good reverb that you know will make that vocal part shine? Why not use one of your own effects Combinators? Want to apply it to your actual audio track? Open the Combinator patch up within the audio track! It's really a very cool way of working. But, it gets even better. This is especially true if you're a producer who really prefers looking at the mixing board, as opposed to the rack.

26. Try this out: Press the F5 button to access the Reason mixer page and locate your Master Channel on the far left. Locate the Sends section of the Master Channel (see Figure 7.24).

Figure 7.24 The Master Channel Send FX section.
Source: Propellerhead Software.

27. Right-click on the Master Channel Send FX Send section and choose Create Send FX → Create Effect (see Figure 7.25).

Figure 7.25 Choosing to Create Effect as a Send Effect.
Source: Propellerhead Software.

28. Now, browse again to the patch folder that you created that houses your new FX Combinator. Once you've selected this patch and have opened it, you'll notice this Combinator is now sitting neatly listed as Combinator 2 in the Send section of your Master Channel. It's now an FX send! From here, you can relabel Combinator 2 as Distortion Reverb, or whatever you want to call it (see Figure 7.26).

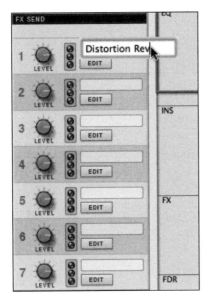

Figure 7.26 Relabeling the Send Label of the Master Channel.
Source: Propellerhead Software.

29. Because we created a Mix Channel and then added our effects Combinator as an insert, you'll also notice that all of those rotaries and buttons that we set up in the Combinator are also appearing on the actual channel strip in the channel next to the Master Channel, as shown in Figure 7.27.

Figure 7.27 The effects Combinator as it appears in the Reason mixer.
Source: Propellerhead Software.

So, not only did we create our own effects device within Reason, but we also re-engineered a Mixer Channel in the actual Reason mixer console! This is absolutely huge, because it affirms that you really do have the same freedom that you have with hardware—except, there is no soldering required.

Conclusion

We made some very big strides in this chapter in the sense that we learned a lot more about programming in Reason, how to make your own hardware, how to engineer knobs and functions in cool ways, and gained insight about some great hardware.

But at the same time, we also brought the rack back around to the mixer. We've got an even bigger insight as to how the rack and mixer are really one, and that you really can move from one part of Reason to another, seamlessly.

We still have one missing element, however, in terms of effects. How do you use MIDI controlled FX? This is a question that will be covered in depth in the next chapter.

Get ready to be introduced to the MIDI controlled effects devices within Reason and learn how to get even better results from them when they are integrated into Combinators/Mix Channels/Audio Tracks.

MIDI Controlled Effects

8

IN THE PAST COUPLE OF CHAPTERS, we've delved into wiring, compiling, and creating your own Reason devices for effects and instruments through Combinator technology. Through these exercises, I hope you've received a good idea of how powerful combining devices and cabling Control Voltages can be, particularly when you know what you're doing.

Now, it's time to continue forward with another set of effects devices that can totally be combined, are powerful on their own, but offer a slightly different way of working. The effects that we've seen, thus far, offer immediate results. You simply plug them in, and you get instant gratification through echoes, reverbs, distortion, and so on. Immediate gratification is good, but there are some cases where if you spend a little extra time on setup, you can get some results that you may have never dreamed possible.

In this chapter, I'll be focusing on devices that either require, or accept, MIDI control from your controller keyboard. A few of these devices will immediately give you the kind of gratification shown by the devices in the last chapter. Some of these devices, however, tend to be overlooked because they aren't initially understood. Not on my watch!

For this chapter, feel free to start off with a new Reason session, as we won't necessarily be using anything from the previous chapters. In this chapter, I would strongly encourage you to pay close attention to the wiring—especially, when we get to the BV512 vocoder. And, if Hip-Hop is the genre of your choosing, you'll want to pay serious attention (see the next section).

Now, with all of the forewarnings out of the way, let's get moving onto MIDI controlled effects within Reason.

Neptune

Who would have known that a simple plug-in that corrects pitch would have changed the music industry as much as Auto-Tune has. By simply plugging in this one simple plug-in, almost any vocalist suddenly becomes radio worthy. So much for raw talent, right?

Reason offers a very similar device to Auto-Tune in the form of Neptune (see Figure 8.1). Not only does the name encapsulate the main job of the device, but it also keeps in line with Propellerhead's growing penchant toward naming instruments after mythological gods. Pretty cool, if you ask me.

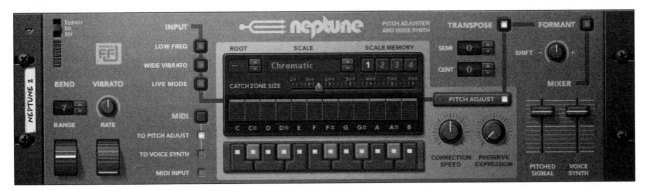

Figure 8.1 The Neptune Pitch Adjuster and Voice Synth.
Source: Propellerhead Software.

But Neptune is no simple "Auto-Tune-ish" device. The pitch correction is really only one feature of this very professional and very interesting device.

Neptune Major Features

Let's start breaking down the major features of Neptune, so that you'll have a better idea of why you may want to use it for your choruses, backing vocals, and straight-up robotic-type effects.

▷ **You can use Neptune as a very natural sounding, pitch correction insert.** If you don't want anyone to know that there was a mistake in the vocal take, you don't have to. Simply choose the desired scale and adjust the Correction Speed value to a moderate level. Suddenly that glaring mistake, in an otherwise perfect take, isn't so glaring.

▷ **Make your vocal tracks sound like the most current hip-hop tracks on the market.** Yes, you can do hard-pitch correction of your voice to emulate your favorite hip-hop act. We'll be covering this particular function in greater detail within the next few pages, so keep reading.

▷ **Instant backing vocals as a Send.** If you add Neptune as a Send effect, Neptune will automatically set itself one octave up. You'll then use the Send knobs to determine how much of the "backing vocals" will be heard.

▷ **You can use Neptune for creating backing vocals.** In Voice Synth mode, you can use Neptune as a sequencer/MIDI controlled harmony device. This is amazing for creating quick multipart harmonies.

Neptune Control Voltage Features

Neptune does have a couple of very unique Control Voltage features: Amplitude and Pitch Control Voltage outputs (see Figure 8.2). These outputs can technically let you use the pitch of a voice, or another monophonic source, to control the pitch through the Pitch adjust section. This can be particularly powerful, but also a little cumbersome. We'll get to this later. Also, it's quite possible to use the Amplitude output to control output levels via voice levels or another source. There are a lot of possibilities!

Figure 8.2 The back panel of Neptune.
Source: Propellerhead Software.

Now that we've gone over Neptune's main functions, let's try it out for size. First, let's check it out as an insert.

Neptune as an Insert (Robotic Style)

To set up a T-Pain, "Robotic-ish," Auto-Tune-style effect, follow these steps:

1. Lay down at least a drumbeat and a bass line that you really like. When finished, apply Neptune as an insert effect to an audio track that is either enabled for monitoring, or is already hosting an audio recording, similar to what you see in Figure 8.3.

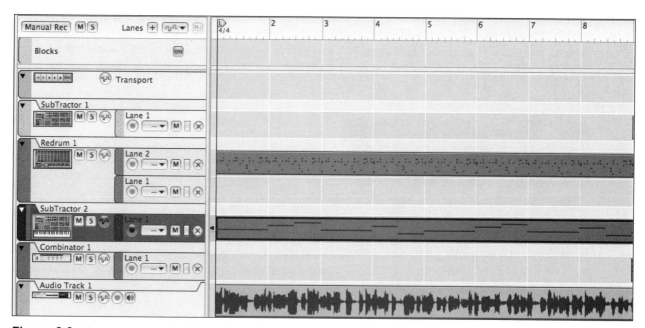

Figure 8.3 An arrangement with vocals in Reason.
Source: Propellerhead Software.

2. Note the keys that your bass line is playing (see Figure 8.4). This is usually the easiest way to determine what keys you'd like to restrict your voice tunings to. If my remark about restricting notes seems confusing, let me explain. Like Auto-Tune, Neptune keeps a monophonic source signal in tune by having the notes that aren't being used eliminated. This process of elimination is done by simply pressing the keys that you *do not* want on its small keyboard, which will cause the small light at the top of the key to darken. Now, if you already know the scale you're singing in, proceed to optional step 3. If not, go directly to step 4 for the note elimination process.

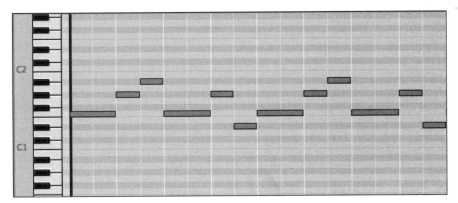

Figure 8.4 A bass line in Reason.
Source: Propellerhead Software.

3. (Optional) Deselect any keys that are not being used by your bass part by pushing the keyboard keys. This will cause the small lights at the top of the notes to go out. Later on, you can add keys that you'd prefer to keep around, but this is just a good starting point. Once you're finished, Neptune will only allow the pitches selected to be heard; any pitch that is off will be either pushed to the nearest key that the original vocal pitch resembles or pushed off to another note (see Figure 8.5).

Figure 8.5 Selected notes for pitch correction in Neptune.
Source: Propellerhead Software.

4. If you know the scale that your voice recording is singing in, choose it by pressing the scale up and down buttons, or simply press inside the scale indicator and a drop-down menu will appear. Once the scale is selected, you'll be able to select the root note on the left (see Figure 8.6).

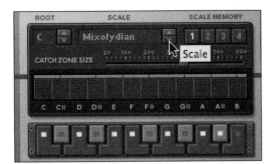

Figure 8.6 Choosing a scale in Neptune.
Source: Propellerhead Software.

5. With the tuning established, it's time to make the proper settings get "robotic." Turn the Correction Speed knob all the way up. This makes Neptune place incoming pitches at exactly the right key with no wiggle room whatsoever. In lower settings, Neptune will gradually pitch parts of an incoming signal, like a vocal part, over to the proper key, as opposed to instantly. You'll also want to make sure that the Preserve Expression knob is down, as shown in Figure 8.7.

Figure 8.7 Correction Speed and Preserve Expression knobs on Neptune.
Source: Propellerhead Software.

And, that's all there is to it! T-Pain effect for the masses within Reason—what's not to like? You can really increase the effect by enabling Formant mode, along with increasing or decreasing the octaves in the Transpose section of Neptune. Try them out and see which settings work best for you. The settings in Figure 8.8 are the ones that worked best for me!

Figure 8.8 Transpose and Formant sections of Neptune.
Source: Propellerhead Software.

Now that we've gotten the robot trick out of the way, let's take a look at using Neptune as a MIDI controlled effect. For this next step, make sure that you keep the Neptune drums, audio, and bass from the last exercise for this next tutorial.

Setting Up a MIDI Controlled Effect

This section is important for all MIDI controlled effects within this chapter. This procedure entails setting up an effect with a sequencer track of its own so that MIDI input can be applied.

To name just one major reason that this is such a cool procedure to put in your memory bank is because you get an extra, tactile ability to use one of these effects in ways that would be most challenging to program. This way, you can use your fingers to make these effects much more versatile because your fingers, through use of a MIDI keyboard, will actually be controlling them—like hardware.

So, to set up a MIDI controlled event, follow these steps.

1. Right-click on Neptune and select Create Track for Neptune 1. This will cause a new sequencer track to appear in the Reason sequencer with a small Neptune icon. It will also be labeled Neptune 1 (see Figure 8.9).

Figure 8.9 Contextual menu for Neptune.
Source: Propellerhead Software.

2. Once the command is executed in the previous step, you'll notice that the sequencer track that appears has a small keyboard underneath the Neptune device (see Figure 8.10). This means that your MIDI keyboard will now have a function over this device. Start your song with the audio recording present within. While it's playing, try playing your MIDI keyboard now.

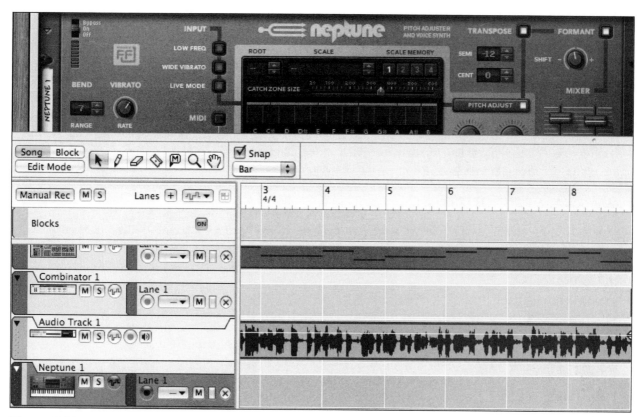

Figure 8.10 Neptune with MIDI Control focus in the Reason sequencer.
Source: Propellerhead Software.

You'll notice that if you hold down the key while in MIDI control of Neptune, any voice (or other type of single note instrument) will instantly snap in pitch to the key you're playing (see Figure 8.11). You now have pitch control of a voice through a keyboard. In the default mode, To Pitch Adjust, you'll only have single note polyphony. But, if you follow on to the next tutorial, you'll learn how to play chords for backing vocals.

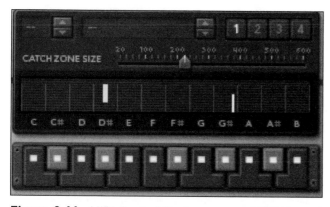

Figure 8.11 MIDI Control Preferences and MIDI Input indicator of Neptune.
Source: Propellerhead Software.

Neptune for Backing Vocals

We can now begin to take a look at one of the other benefits of the Neptune device: its harmonizing ability. Through the use of the Voice Synth function, it's possible to gain some very convincing, and very elaborate, harmonies in your song by simply holding notes on a keyboard.

It's important to note that while Neptune is in Voice Synth mode, it actually still does its original job of pitch correction. With that being said, go ahead and set up your pitch correction first. But know that when you use the Voice Synth mode, you lose the ability to adjust the pitch of the main voice with a MIDI keyboard. Again, pitch correction is still occurring, but it's just Neptune controlling it, not you.

To enable the Voice Synth mode and play harmonies polyphonically, try the following:

1. Toggle to Voice Synth mode in the MIDI section of Neptune (see Figure 8.12). Once this mode is enabled, you will be able to sustain multiple notes through holding multiple keys down on the Neptune's sequencer track with a MIDI focus.

Figure 8.12 The MIDI section of Neptune set in Voice Synth mode.
Source: Propellerhead Software.

2. You'll note that the lead, or original pitch-corrected voice, is still going in the foreground. If you want the backup harmonies to be lower, simply lower the Voice Synth mixer level slightly, or make it significantly lower than the pitched signal (see Figure 8.13). The Pitched Signal slider is the original voice, in case you just want the backup vocals and not the original recording.

Figure 8.13 The Mixer section of Neptune with the Voice Synth level lowered.
Source: Propellerhead Software.

Conclusion to Neptune

If your head isn't swimming with possibilities for Neptune, you're either a very skilled do-it natural vocalist, or you have access to a professional choir. This is a very powerful piece of kit, especially if you're like me and only have mediocre vocal abilities, at best. Use this device, and people really will think you have serious vocal abilities. End of story.

Now it's time to take a look at a very distant cousin of Neptune, the BV512 Vocoder.

BV512 Vocoder

The BV512 Vocoder has actually been in Reason for some time, and technically isn't a MIDI controlled effect in the way that you would think (see Figure 8.14). But it is *still* a MIDI controlled effect. The place where a keyboard can control the vocoder is through the opening and closing of bands, which I'll expand on later in this chapter. I mention this now so that you'll know that the MIDI controlled effect is not for manipulating voice pitch, which is the classic vocoder scenario.

Figure 8.14 The BV512 Vocoder.
Source: Propellerhead Software.

Vocoders are tricky devices that aren't difficult to use, if you understand how they work. If you don't, though, you'll be scratching your head for a while. Or you'll simply move on, and never really get a glimpse at how cool this device really is!

Vocoders are responsible for many of the robot voices heard in shows like *Battlestar Galactica, Transformers,* and many others. They have also seen a heavy resurgence over the past decade within the techno, trance, dubstep, hip-hop, and other genres.

The BV512 vocoder in Reason actually works exactly the same as the hardware. And, in this case, it's a blessing and a curse. To even get the vocoder functional, you actually have a few cables you'll need to connect to specific devices before it will work. Simply just creating a BV512 will not accomplish anything. As a matter of fact, this is probably the most finicky of all the Reason devices to get working. Once the device is set up, though, you can have hours of fun making robot voices, choirs, and so on.

The way the vocoder works is like this: It takes one signal that's coming in, which is usually a vocal source, and uses this signal to modulate what's known as a carrier signal. This carrier signal is usually a synthesizer or any device that can maintain a constant signal. Basically, you need to have lots of whole notes going into the carrier input.

The tricky part is this: You need to have both the modulator and the carrier signal going at once, in order for you to hear the effect of the vocoder. In the past, this was kind of tough because Reason had no real-time recording. Now that it does, you can do real-time vocoding!

Let's go over some of the BV512's major features now.

Major Features

The BV512 has several little tricks that you can use. These are some of the main features, as they apply to vocoding and equalization.

▷ **Up to 512 frequency bands of vocoding.** You can emulate the old vocoders by restricting frequency bands, and you can also have very clear and succinct vocoding where source voices going through the vocoder are intelligible. Take it from me, you can make some killer alien voices with any of the band modes.

▷ **Unique Hold feature.** The Hold button on the BV512 is unique in the sense that it allows you to actually pause filter setting of the Vocoder, while still letting the carrier signal pass through. To put this in English, you can freeze a modulator formant of a voice, while the carrier signal (a synth) is still changing the pitch around. You can get some really good leads with this feature.

▷ **Optional Equalizer mode.** You can switch the BV512 over to EQ mode, and just like the knob implies, you suddenly have a graphic EQ.

▷ **Possible spectral analyzer.** It's not a true spectral analyzer, but you can actually visually see what the frequencies in a signal are doing with the BV512 display. Simply route an audio signal to the modulator input. Instantly, you'll see the frequencies in the display. Furthermore, you can increase the amount of bands being used all the way up to 512 to get an even more accurate picture.

The Back Panel

The BV512 has quite a few CV possibilities, starting with the individual band level ins and outs (see Figure 8.15). Using the outputs allows you to have certain bands modulate parameters of other devices. For example, a low band can trigger the gate input of a Redrum device, thus using a voice to cause a bass drum to be triggered. Pretty cool, especially if you're a beat boxer.

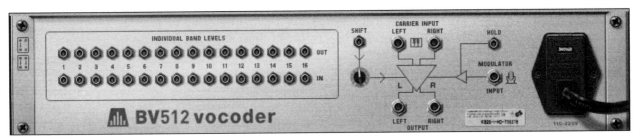

Figure 8.15 The back panel of the BV512 vocoder.
Source: Propellerhead Software.

The Band CV inputs allow you to use external modulation sources from other Reason devices to trigger different bands. I could use the same example above with Redrum, but in reverse. Imagine Redrum gate outputs rhythmically opening and closing bands while a voice traveled through as a modulator. The possibilities are staggering.

While I'm back here, showing you different inputs and outputs, let me point out two very important inputs and outputs. First, I'll start with the Modulator Input, as shown in Figure 8.16

Figure 8.16 BV512 Modulator Input.
Source: Propellerhead Software.

Notice that there is a small picture of a microphone next to it. This is where you'll plug in the output of your audio track, your voice, or someone else's voice. The synthesizer goes into the Carrier Input; notice how there's a small keyboard next to this input (see Figure 8.17).

Figure 8.17 BV512 Carrier Input.
Source: Propellerhead Software.

I point these inputs out, because they are the most important part of making the vocoder work. If these are plugged in, along with the vocoder outputs, you'll be making robot voices until the cows come home. Should you forget? Well, you'll be spending some extra time routing.

A few other CV inputs I'd like to point out would be the Hold Input and the Shift Input, which can be seen in Figure 8.15. The Hold Input obviously affects the Hold button on the front. This is a really interesting function, in the sense that it holds the frequency bands open on the vocoder in the exact position in which the modulator left them. If you can imagine modulating a function like this, you'll notice that there are some very cool possibilities for stutter and hanging effects within vocoded vocals, drums, and so on. One possibility is to use a Matrix Curve to introduce random holds.

Secondly, the Shift knob "shifts" the carrier frequencies up and down. If you're using the vocoder for typical voice/robotic effects processing, it sounds very much like you're shifting the voice up and down. You can get some cool voice processing with this, especially when you take it down a few steps. Try modulating with slow Sine Wave LFO from a Thor, and you'll get some creepy voice modulation that you won't soon forget.

Now that you have a good understanding of the BV512 back panel, let's try to actually set up the vocoder in one of the most classic setups.

Setting Up the Classic Vocoder Effect (More Robot)

For this exercise, let's go ahead and start with a new Reason session, but again, with a drumbeat and a vocal track. (This part is more for you than me. You need rhythm, right?) We'll add the synthesizer in as we go along. Once you've got a drumbeat and a vocal recording that spans at least 8 measures, proceed to step 1.

1. Hold down the Shift button on your keyboard and create a BV512 vocoder as an insert in the audio track that hosts your vocal recording (see Figure 8.18). Holding down the Shift button will keep the Reason cables from auto-routing. And, believe me, in this particular configuration, the auto-routing will not work because it won't set up the vocals as the modulator automatically.

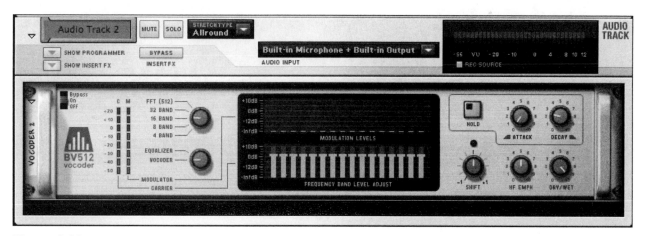

Figure 8.18 The BV512 Vocoder as an insert.
Source: Propellerhead Software.

2. Now, let's set the cabling up the right way for vocal vocoding. Send the Left To Device output to the BV512 Modulator Input (see Figure 8.19). This sets up the actual audio signal as to what will eventually modulate a synthesizer.

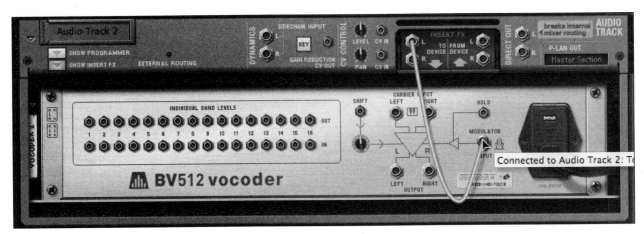

Figure 8.19 The To Device Left output routed to the Modulator Input of the BV512.
Source: Propellerhead Software.

3. This next part is highly important and often missed, which means that people usually end up scratching their heads and never using the vocoder again. Don't make this mistake! Always remember to set up an output from the BV512, or you'll never hear your vocoded signal! Route the Carrier Output of the BV512 vocoder to the From Device Input on the Audio Track device (see Figure 8.20). Left only!

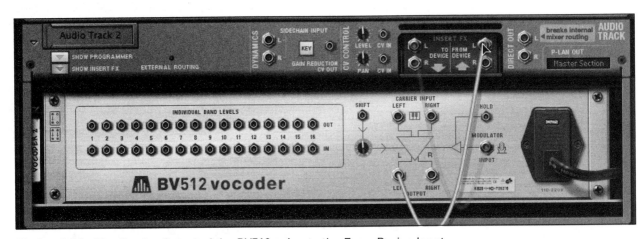

Figure 8.20 The Carrier Output of the BV512 going to the From Device Input.
Source: Propellerhead Software.

4. Here comes the fun part: setting up the Carrier, which is going to be a Subtractor. Right-click on the BV512 and create a Subtractor synthesizer; make sure it's initialized. You'll notice that you can actually fit the Subtractor into the Audio Track internal rack as an insert (see Figure 8.21). This is something that should give you quite a bit of room for ideas going forward, as this really opens up the kind of effects engineering you can do with audio involving synthesizer CVs and plain ordinary usage. You'll also notice that the Subtractor will perfectly auto-route itself to the Carrier Left Input on the BV512.

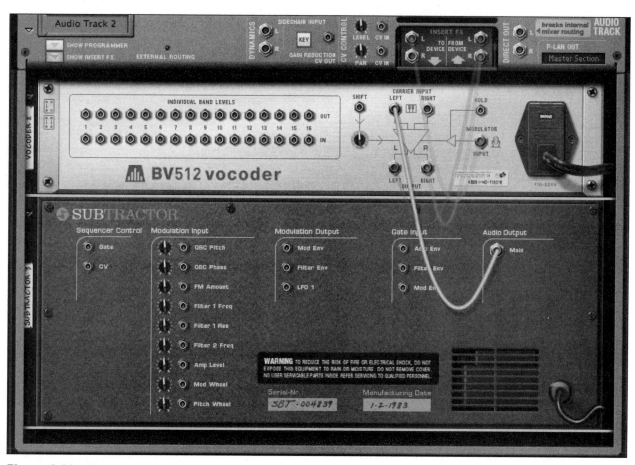

Figure 8.21 The Subtractor added to an Audio Track as an insert and carrier for the BV512.
Source: Propellerhead Software.

5. Here's where we get to a personal decision for you. Do you want the synthesizer to run automatically, without having to play it? Or do you want to actually play the synthesizer and have direct control over the pitch of your vocoded vocals with your fingertips? For actual MIDI control of the Subtractor, proceed to step 7. If you'd like to go without having to play the synthesizer, simply insert a Matrix pattern sequencer by right-clicking on the Subtractor and creating a Matrix from the Utilities section of the Create menu. Set up the Matrix pattern in either 1/8 or 1/4 resolution and tie all of the notes so that the carrier is a seamless stream. Notice in Figure 8.22 how I have a 1/4 note resolution with many tied notes in a pattern.

Figure 8.22 The Matrix added as an insert to control a Subtractor synthesizer in 1/4 resolution.
Source: Propellerhead Software.

6. When making your Matrix pattern, I would advise programming in a lower octave, simply because this is where vocoding sounds very cool. But feel free to experiment. If you've already started a pattern and don't want to shift down, simply lower the octave of the oscillator on the Subtractor as I have done with Oscillator 1 with a setting of 3. You'll note that I've also enabled Oscillator 2 and have kept the Octave at 4. By having two oscillators at two different octaves, I'm able to give the perception of a "fatter" carrier signal. I've also opened up the Filter on the Subtractor so that the signal coming out is a little brighter. Modify this to your taste, of course. Finally, the most important part when using a step sequencer to control a carrier signal, increase your Amp Envelope Sustain all the way up. Remember, the carrier signal directly affects how loud your signal is (see Figure 8.23). If the carrier signal drops out over time, due to a low sustain level from your synth, your vocoder vocals will continually and gradually fade out. You'll also want to set your polyphony to 1. You can get some note overlap when having this many tied notes on a Matrix, but this will fix the issue and keep your carrier signal pretty and tight.

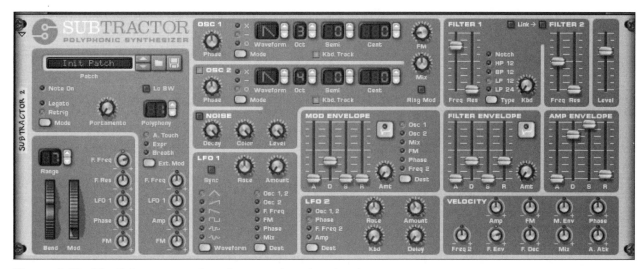

Figure 8.23 The Subtractor settings for a good carrier signal.
Source: Propellerhead Software.

7. With the Subtractor set up, we should now take a look at the BV512's own settings. For the most comprehensible vocoder setting, it's about going with the 512 FFT setting. In this mode, you can basically discern anything being said, but it's still highly vocoded. However, if you want something a little more vintage, I'd highly suggest exploring the lower band settings. The only drawback of going with all 512 bands is that you're adding on a latency between your audio track and the actual vocoding process. This can be mended easily by taking off your Snap in the sequencer and just pushing the audio back a hair. Personally, the latency has only been marginal on my end, so I usually leave it where it is. Next, I usually remove any attack and release on my vocoder settings. The release, in particular, causes the filter bands to stay open slightly longer, making the carrier signal take just a little longer to go away. In order to keep the vocals clear, I usually opt to take this off and add on a little delay later if I want some effect with my vocoders. As you can see in Figure 8.24, I also roll off a little of the low end. Remember, we're using a synthesizer going through a low-pass filter for our carrier signal, so it does carry a bit of bass. I can also take care of this in the mixer screen, but because I can also see which bands are being modulated the heaviest, it doesn't hurt to take care of it at the source. The HF Emph, or high frequency emphasis, should be sparingly rolled back on a case-by-case basis. Too much can add a lot of sibilance and high frequency noise to your vocoded vocals. Too little can make you sound like a robot with an inferiority complex—meaning that you'll only be able to hear the low end, and it will be harder to make out what is being said. And, finally, I pull back just a hair on the Shift knob to about -6. With the bands being shifted lower, it gives the impression that my voice is lower than it is, without adjusting the carrier frequency.

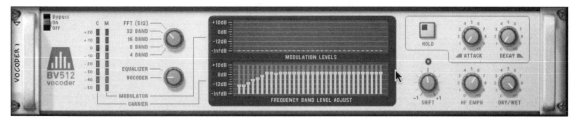

Figure 8.24 Basic BV512 settings for a nice robot.
Source: Propellerhead Software.

8. If you've elected to actually play the pitches supplied by the Subtractor synthesizer, and you've already set up the Subtractor settings in step 7, why don't you set it up where the Subtractor can be MIDI controlled while acting as an insert for your audio track (see Figure 8.25). Right-click on the Subtractor and choose Create Track for Subtractor. Instantly, a track will appear in the sequencer with MIDI focus on a Subtractor. As soon as you push the Start button, or the Play button, try holding down notes on your keyboard. You should be hearing pitched, robotic vocals now. Very cool stuff.

Figure 8.25 Setting up the Subtractor to be MIDI controlled while acting as an insert device.
Source: Propellerhead Software.

Now that you've gotten the basic functionality of the BV512 down, and you understand what is MIDI and what is modulation and carrier signal, let's move on to another piece of amazing kit.

Let's have a look at the Alligator.

Alligator

The Alligator is a nasty beast, indeed. And, it's not technically just one device, it has several things going on at once (see Figure 8.26). But, it's main purpose is that it is a triple filtered gate.

Figure 8.26 The Alligator.
Source: Propellerhead Software.

The Alligator is designed to take a boring signal, like a pad, and turn it into something rhythmic and wild. It has a built-in pattern sequencer that generates several different combinations of the gates opening and closing. Each gate also has several different variables that can be used to individualize the sound from the two other gates hiding within the Alligator. This means that from one boring pad, you can actually create three different rhythmic synths playing in perfect synchronization.

This device is, by far, the most instant gratification you will get from any effect within Reason. It just makes everything sound danceable and good. If you like any form of Pop music, Electronica, or would like to do some amazing gating to a guitar, you'll want to spend some time here.

Like all the other effects in this chapter, it is also MIDI controllable. Rather than having to use the built-in pattern generator, you can also trigger the gates with a MIDI controller. This can be a lot of fun for gating voices, drums, and anything else you can think of. Whatever you use it for, it's always a memorable effect.

Let's go over the major features now.

Major Features

▷ **Three highly programmable gates.** The Alligator multiplexes three signals from one stereo incoming signal. These three signals go through three different gates simultaneously that can be opened and closed rhythmically with a MIDI keyboard or the built-in pattern generator.

▷ **Built-in pattern generator**. There is an optional built-in pattern generator that can be used to rhythmically trigger each gate for you. By default, this function is in the On position, so you'll hear it in action as soon as you create an Alligator for your Reason instrument or audio track. There is also a Resolution knob to control how fast the pattern generator plays in reference to the host clock. And there's a Shift knob to offset the pattern.

▷ **Three filters.** On each filter, there is a different filter type. For example, Filter 1 has a High Pass filter, where Filter 3 has a Low Pass. You can adjust the filter settings to make each gate unique from the others. It can almost make it sound like you've added three different instruments to your arrangement from one device source signal. You can also elect to disable each filter with the Filter On/Off buttons located on each gate.

▷ **One ADR envelope to govern pattern characteristics.** The AMP envelope of the Alligator lets you sculpt how the gates open and close. This can be quite cool, in the sense that you can ultimately sculpt how the incoming signal goes in and out of the Alligator. Do you want the three gates to be choppy or have a slight release?

▷ **Synced delay.** One, or all, of your gates can be routed through the delay module nestled toward the bottom of the Alligator. By adding effects to select gates, you can greatly differentiate between the different gates and what they are doing.

▷ **Phaser.** Similar to the synced delay, the phaser can be routed to one and all of the gated channels within the Alligator. Use the phaser to add some of the ethereal elements to your gated audio.

▷ **Assignable filter envelope.** The filter envelope can be assigned to one, or all, of the different gates in incremental amounts. It's possible through one basic tone to make one Alligator gate sound like a lead, where another sounds like a bass, by having the filter in full effect on the low pass gate with the filter envelope. Then, with the high pass gate, have little to absolutely no filter and filter envelope.

▷ **Built-in mixer functionality.** You can control Pan and Volume for each gate of the Alligator. This leads to additional possibilities in customizing and creating new grooves. The mixer also acts as the conduit for choosing how much delay, distortion, and phaser are added to your three gated channels.

▷ **Assignable LFO.** Like the filter envelope, you can also assign incremental LFO, in both positive and negative polarities, to either one, or all, of the filters on each Alligator gate. Again, this is another of the many ways to customize your Alligator patch. One great example of how to use this setting would be to assign a small amount of LFO modulation to the High Pass filter, with its LFO setting set to a negative polarity setting. This will cause the high pass gated part to swoop in and out of audible range, giving more of a fade-in and fade-out effect.

▷ **Assignable drive/distortion.** In addition to Phaser and Delay as built-in effects, you may also add distortion to individual, or all of the channels within the Alligator through the use of the Drive knobs. These knobs are located on each of the gate channels and are more than capable of creating severe separation between each gated part coming from the Alligator.

Control Voltage and Audio I/O Functionality

As I mentioned in the functionality rundown, the Alligator actually created three more parts out of one source input. Thankfully, there are individual audio outputs for each gate, as shown in Figure 8.27, so that you can individually affect each part as much as you'd like from within the Reason mixer.

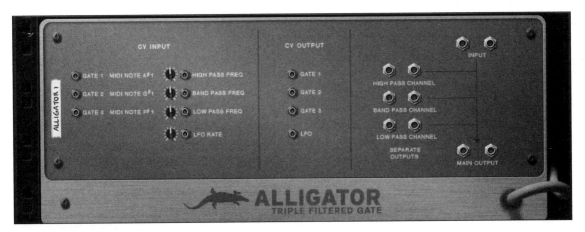

Figure 8.27 The Alligator back panel.
Source: Propellerhead Software.

On the CV end of things, there are many possibilities. You get CV outputs from each gate. This can be a little more fun than you might imagine. The CV outputs send pulses from the built-in Pattern Generator on the Alligator when it's on. Using the CV outputs in this respect can allow you to use the Alligator as a drum computer, as one example. Try connecting each gate output into individual gate inputs on a Redrum drum computer and then listen to the beats that are created. It's actually pretty cool.

You can use the Gate Inputs on the Alligator, as one example, to have a secondary sequencer, like a Matrix, control the pattern of gate opening, as opposed to the internal pattern generator. This will allow you to create custom gate patterns, as opposed to generic.

One small part you might not think about is the fact that there is a CV input for the LFO rate of the Alligator. Try using a Pulveriser's Follower, assigned to be modulated by a kick drum to modulate the LFO rate of your Alligator, which is modulating a synth. You can get some wicked rhythms this way.

Now that we have a good idea of the front and back panel functionality of the Alligator, let's try having it chew up some audio as an insert.

Using the Alligator as an Insert with MIDI Control

For this final exercise, let's experience the Alligator in a way that shows you how powerful it really is—through its simplicity. For this exercise, we'll be starting from a new session.

1. In a new Reason session, set up a drumbeat with a Redrum drum computer, a Dr. Octo Rex, or a Kong Drum Module. Create a beat or load up a beat (Dr. Octo Rex) that suits your style, mood, or genre. Next, create a Thor synthesizer and load up any patch that suits your fancy and is capable of sustained notes. I'd recommend a patch like Big String Synth from the Pad directory for Thor in the Reason Factory Sound Bank. Record a nice, sustained 1/2 note to 1/4 note melody. The sustained notes are perfect to hear the power of the Alligator. When ready, set the sequence up on a sequencer loop, see Figure 8.28. The Alligator is a very tweakable device, and what's more tweakable than a drum synth loop?

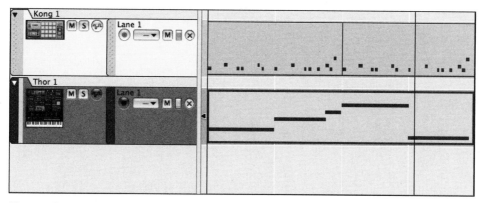

Figure 8.28 Basic drum and synth arrangement.
Source: Propellerhead Software.

2. Here's the fun part: drop in an Alligator by right-clicking on the Thor Mix Channel device and creating an Alligator (see Figure 8.29). It works best to do this while the sequence is playing. As soon as you start to hear the chopping, try adjusting through the different pattern numbers to get a feel for what's available.

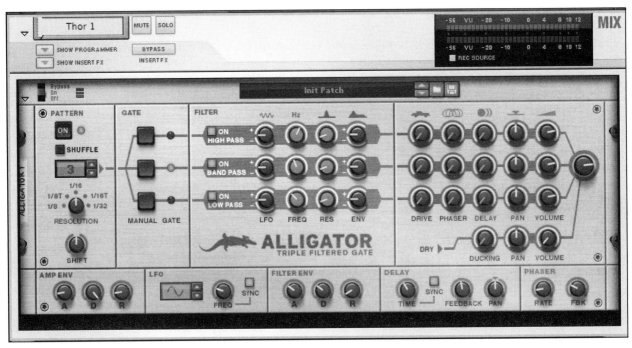

Figure 8.29 The Alligator as an insert effect.
Source: Propellerhead Software.

3. Now, try adjusting the Amp Envelope settings, particularly the D, or Decay, of the Alligator's gates (see Figure 8.30). This, along with the R, or Release, will help you mold what the gates are doing. Do you want a rhythmic pad? Do you want some staccato synth sounds, or do you want a gated pad? Try modifying these settings and notice how much of a change you can make from that original, sustained pad.

Figure 8.30 The Amp Envelope section of the Alligator.
Source: Propellerhead Software.

4. This would also be a good time to try different patterns at different resolution settings, or the speed of the patterns in relation to the host clock (see Figure 8.31). You'll find that through the combination of patterns, Amp Envelope settings, and resolution settings, there are far more patterns than the perceived 64 included patterns. Through the changing of resolutions, one pattern becomes an entirely different one. Through adjusting the Attack, Decay, and Release settings of the Amp Envelope, the patterns become even more unique. Finally, in this step, try shifting the pattern with the Shift knob. This modifies where the pattern starts, offsetting the pattern and giving the overall pattern a different vibe.

Figure 8.31 The Pattern section of the Alligator.
Source: Propellerhead Software

5. But wait, there are even more possibilities in terms of pattern modification. Try adjusting the Volume and Pan knobs, and switch between patterns, as shown in Figure 8.32. Note how changing the volume can directly affect the perceived rhythm of the Alligator's patterns. This is the point where the light bulb should appear over your head, notifying you that you have a huge trunk of inspiration here with the Alligator. If you need a quick bass line, or if you need a filler part to add some spice to your song, the Alligator can really fill things up quickly, if you give it a chance.

Figure 8.32 The Volume and Pan knobs for the three gates of the Alligator.
Source: Propellerhead Software.

6. Another thing that really should be experienced with the Alligator is that at any point, you can revert to your original part before it went into the Alligator. For example, we have a pad right now that is reasonably cool. We could keep that pad going through the Alligator while vocals are taking place, but when an instrumental section of the song comes up, bring the pad back. How? By using the Volume knob in the Dry section, shown in Figure 8.33. It's also possible to have the original part, in this case, a pad, and the Alligator-gated part, playing side by side. Simply place the Dry knob halfway or somewhere that sounds good to you. With the Pan knob next to the Volume knob, you can even choose where the original part will lie within the stereo field. Finally, the Ducking knob will duck the original part based on the Amp Envelope settings, basically giving you a fourth gate! Try bringing the Dry knob up to about 75% and then raising and lowering the Decay while the Ducking knob is at 75% as well. Notice how the dry pattern is also affected by what the Amp Envelope settings are doing while the Ducking knob is active.

Figure 8.33 The Dry section of the Alligator.
Source: Propellerhead Software.

7. Drop the Dry Volume and Ducking back down now, and let's take a look at how the Alligator can be MIDI controlled. Go ahead and repeat the familiar step that has been repeated throughout this chapter, where you right-click on the Alligator and choose Create Track for Alligator 1. This would also be a good time to turn off the Pattern section so that the built-in patterns no longer play (see Figure 8.34). Simply press the On button to do this, the light next to it will shut off, and when you play your sequence, you'll just hear nothing.

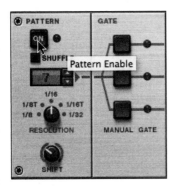

Figure 8.34 Turning the Pattern section off on the Alligator.
Source: Propellerhead Software.

8. Let's try playing the Alligator now! On your MIDI controller, move down to the C1 octave and locate F#1, G#1, and A#1. These are the three keys that are assigned to the Gates of the Alligator (see Figure 8.35). Try running your sequence now, and while it's running, press these keys. Notice how you can now create rhythms of your own using your own fingers.

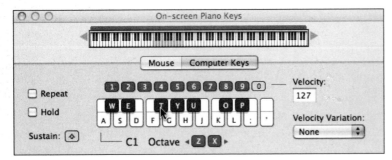

Figure 8.35 The On-screen Piano Keys of Reason with my mouse cursor showing where the Gate keys of the Alligator start.
Source: Propellerhead Software.

Conclusion

There you have it, a big walk-through of a fascinating kind of device within Reason where your fingers can have another kind of effect on sound, as opposed to only pitch. And you've also been introduced to devices that greatly inspire music making with their modern sound and thoughtful design. If you followed all of these exercises through to the end, I'm confident that you'll be swimming with new ideas.

All of the sections in this chapter have exercises that describe the most common ways to use these devices. So, if you ever feel the need to get back to how we did something before, just come back here and try it again. In fact, the whole book is written this way.

I hope that by going through the exercises within this book, you've got what you need for your project or studio when it comes to Reason. It really is an all-in-one, virtual studio that is unique and comprehensive. Through all my years of using it, I always find myself coming back to it and exploring it. It really is like an old, well-used piece of hardware in my studio that I can always rely on due to its sound and stability. And when you throw all those attributes together, you'll find that it all equals one word: irreplaceable.

Rack Extensions

N ow, LET'S TALK ABOUT what the .5 is for in Reason 6.5. You might think it's something small, like a new MIDI feature, or, something even more obscure. But, actually, it's a really huge step for Reason, in general. And, if you're new to Reason…well, you came at the right moment.

Reason 6.5 adds a new technology to the Reason rack. This new technology finally allows third-party developers to make Reason instruments, effects, and devices for the notoriously closed, virtual studio. This really is a huge step because you can finally customize your rack in a way that truly makes it yours. And because the products made available by other companies are tightly controlled by Propellerhead, you can rest assured that Reason will remain as stable as it always has in the past.

Let me give you an example. Korg, a music company well known for its synthesizers, tuners, Kaossilators, and more, designed a Rack Extension device that emulates their classic synth, the Polysix (discussed later in this chapter in the Korg Polysix section). This is an amazing, virtual model of the synthesizer that you can use within Reason, just like any other Reason device (see Figure 9.1).

Figure 9.1 The Korg Polysix.
Source: Korg.

And this is just one of the pieces of virtual gear that you can buy for Reason!

VST/AU?

Reason still does *not* allow AU or VST plug-ins. Rack Extensions is a proprietary software design that only works with Reason. But because this design is Reason specific, there are some advantages that VST, AU (audio units), or RTAS, and so on would never have provided.

We'll talk about those advantages in the next section. But while there are thousands of amazing plug-ins out there within these formats, there are dangers when it comes to adding them into a host software. These dangers are mainly in the form of bugs and crashes, which ultimately compromise the stability of the host program—in this case, Reason. Also, extensive testing is done on each RE before it is made available for sale, as well as CPU optimization.

Reason has been known for years to be one of the most reliable software packages on the market, as well as one of the most CPU efficient. And this is something that Reason's developers have always been aware of and eager to maintain. Developing their own format may seem haughty from a distance, but when you consider it's a successful effort to maintain a highly stable and complex software studio...it does make sense.

The Reason Back Panel

One of the key features of the Reason rack has always been the way that you could turn the rack around by pressing the Tab button and then re-route Control Voltages, audio cables, and so on. With Rack Extensions, you'll find that third-party instruments, effects, and other devices now get the same treatment. Third-party developers are able to set up the same kinds of audio inputs and outputs and CV inputs and outputs that we all know and love with the classic Reason devices.

And like we learned in the Combinator chapter, because each new Reason device can add new Control Voltage and audio features to a rack and a Combinator, buying one new Rack Extension device could add a new feature that you, or Propellerhead, may never have thought of adding to Reason.

For example, Rob Papen's Predator synthesizer has a much more elaborate arpeggiator than RPG-8, which is included in Reason. Predator also has Control Voltage outputs coming from its own built-in arpeggiator (see Figure 9.2). Because you can use the Predator arpeggiator outputs to trigger other Reason devices, you haven't just bought a synthesizer, you've also bought a new arpeggiator as well! That's just one of the things that Predator adds to your rack.

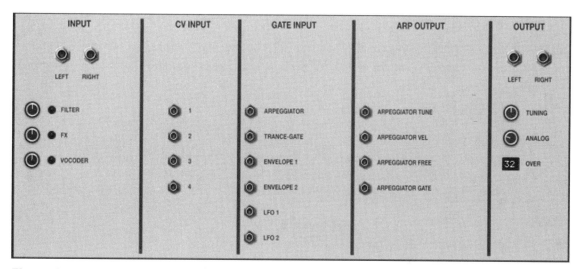

Figure 9.2 Predator, from Rob Papen.
Source: Rob Papen Soundware.

This synthesizer also adds many more capabilities to Reason with functionality, processing, and Control Voltages. But this is just one device. Many more are being added all the time. From now on, the tricks that were always somewhat universal with Control Voltages, audio routing, Combinator creation, and so on will be evolving at a much faster rate than they were before.

In the past, we always had to rely on an update for Reason to add more Control Voltage tricks. Now, it occurs every time a new device is added. And you may have a device that someone else doesn't have! The tricks will continually be evolving now, and you can be a part of them.

So where do you get Rack Extensions? How do you manage them?

Getting New Rack Extensions

Normally, you wouldn't think that a pro level book would do any hand-holding in this area of discovery. But downloading, managing, and purchasing Rack Extensions can be a little confusing at first. I thought I'd devote at least a small section to it, so you aren't banging your head against the wall when you decide you want to pick up some REs for yourself.

RE—Rack Extensions

Throughout this chapter, I'll use the terms Rack Extensions and REs interchangeably.

First, let's talk about what's involved with installing REs.

Installing Rack Extensions

Actually, Reason installs Rack Extensions for you, so you don't have to worry about running an installer or anything like that. Also, you can try the full, working version of any RE within the Propellerhead store for 30 days before you decide whether you want to buy it.

1. Go to the Shop at Propellerhead.com (see Figure 9.3).

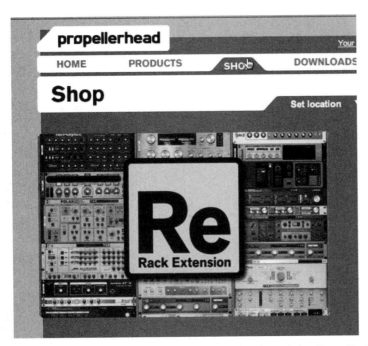

Figure 9.3 Click on Shop in the navigation bar of the Propellerhead store.
Source: Propellerhead Software.

2. Select Rack Extensions, as shown in Figure 9.4.

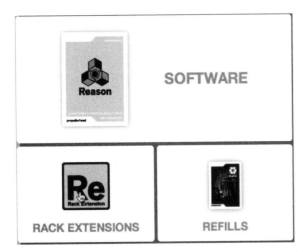

Figure 9.4 Select the Rack Extensions section, which is also marked with RE.
Source: Propellerhead Software.

3. Choose to either Try or Buy the RE of your choice. Try is instant, and requires no more action (see Figure 9.5). Buy, of course, will prompt you to enter your payment info, etc.

Figure 9.5 Try or Buy an RE in the Propellerhead shop.
Source: Propellerhead Software.

4. Once you've either tried or bought Authorizer, a Propellerhead application will begin downloading and installing your new RE (see Figure 9.6). This is separate from your Web browser.

Figure 9.6 Authorizer, as it downloads and installs an RE.
Source: Propellerhead Software.

5. When it's finished, you'll be prompted to restart Reason (see Figure 9.7). The RE will not work until you restart. In fact, it won't even be visible.

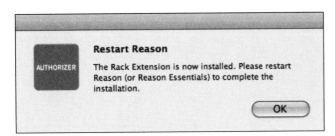

Figure 9.7 The prompt to restart Reason after an RE is installed.
Source: Propellerhead Software.

6. Once you restart Reason, you'll have to go to the Create menu and then right-click the contextual menu or the Device Palette page of the Tool window, in order to see your new purchase, or trial instrument, device, effect, etc. (see Figure 9.8).

Figure 9.8 The Tool window of Reason with my new RE.
Source: Propellerhead Software.

As you can see, it's a little different from how you would normally install a plug-in type device. But it's also really simple, requires no work on your part, and is extremely quick.

Also, the fact that your Rack Extension devices show up in the Create/Contextual/Tool window, along with all the other Reason devices, ensures that all your devices stay organized and available for easy use.

Rack Extension Organization

Rack Extensions do appear in the same places that you create, or select, all other Reason devices, but they are also categorized into the groups where they make the most sense. For example, if I Try or Buy a new synthesizer RE, it will appear in the Instruments submenu of the Create menu. If I Try or Buy a more esoteric effect, like Etch (a filter bank, with LFOs), it will appear in Creative Effects. Just because you don't see it in the first menu where you look, doesn't mean it's not there.

When "Tried" REs Expire

After 30 days, when you try an RE, it will eventually disappear out of your list of Reason devices that you created. There won't be an annoying message stating that such and such has expired. It will just cease to exist.

Now, here's the kicker: If you have a song that uses a particular RE, and the RE is expired, it means that your trial is up. Or if you have deleted the device, for whatever reason, you'll get the error message shown in Figure 9.9.

Figure 9.9 Reason error message, letting you know that a Rack Extension is missing or has expired.
Source: Propellerhead Software.

You will also have a little cardboard box-looking device in your Reason rack where the missing device should be (see Figure 9.10). If you press in the indicated area on the box, it will state "Click here to go to the Propellerhead shop and get it."

Figure 9.10 The lovely cardboard box that Reason gives you in place of a missing RE.
Source: Propellerhead Software.

Propellerhead has set up a nice, comfy situation where you can enjoy many different REs before you buy them. But nothing is more annoying than being unable to run a song because you haven't purchased a particular device or effect. Therefore, I do have a bit of advice on the topic.

If you'd like to keep your songs intact with "Tried" REs, bounce the track that uses the RE to an audio track before the Rack Extension expires.

This can be done by going to the File menu in Reason and selecting Bounce Mixer Channels (see Figure 9.11).

Figure 9.11 Bounce Mixer Channels as it appears in the Reason File menu.
Source: Propellerhead Software.

If the RE that you have on trial is an effect, keep in mind that it will not appear in the Bounce Mixer Channels window as an option to bounce. In my case, Buffre, the RE that I'd like to capture, is an effect, not an instrument. The instrument that it is running through is actually the Polysix from Korg. I'll go ahead and check off the Polysix in the Bounce Mixer Channels window, letting Reason know that this is the track to export. Because the Polysix is going through Buffre as an effect, it will still retain the Buffre effect in the finished audio track (see Figure 9.12).

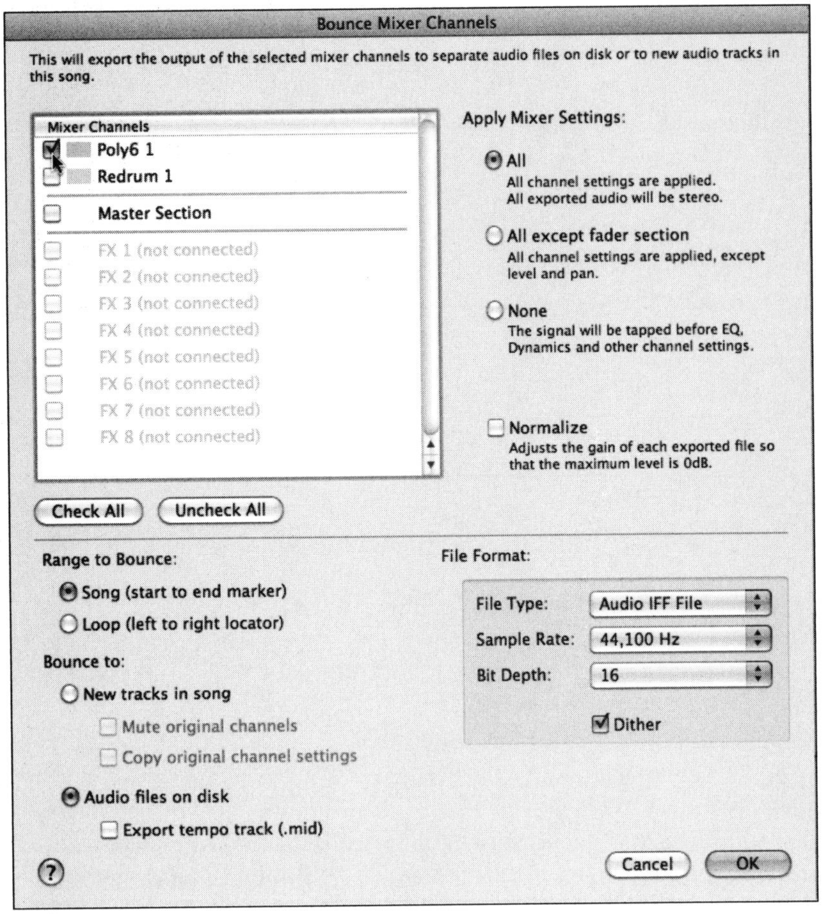

Figure 9.12 The Polysix selected in the Bounce Mixer Channels window of Reason.
Source: Propellerhead Software.

It's also very important that I select the "Bounce to: New tracks in song" option within the Bounce Mixer Channels options. This will place the captured audio with the RE effect (in this case, instrument, device, etc.) into the Reason sequencer as an audio file (see Figure 9.13).

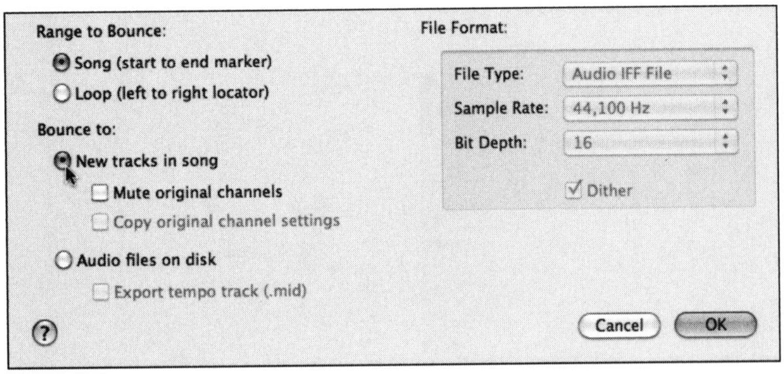

Figure 9.13 "Bounce to: New tracks in song" option for capturing RE effect.
Source: Propellerhead Software.

After I press the OK button in the Bounce Mixer Channels menu, Reason will go to town, rendering my RE audio along with the instrument and everything pertinent (see Figure 9.14).

Figure 9.14 Reason's rendering in action.
Source: Propellerhead Software.

After the rendering is complete, I can look in my sequencer window and note that there is a Polysix 1 Bounced audio file that appears as a track, as shown in Figure 9.15.

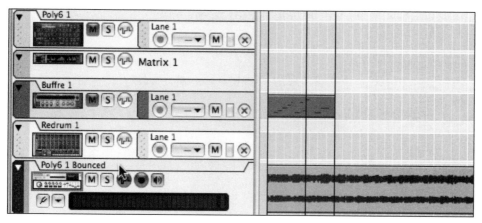

Figure 9.15 Polysix as a Bounced audio file in the Reason sequencer.
Source: Propellerhead Software.

You'll notice in the sequencer page, I muted the Polysix and Buffre. I don't need them playing over the bounce audio. In fact, I can delete them now. Of course, before bouncing, you will want to ensure that you are finished with the work you want to do with the trial RE. Remember, it won't be there when you come back—unless you purchase it.

This brings up another question. How do you keep track of how long you have left with an RE?

Checking the Expiration Dates on Your REs

There's a really easy way to keep tabs on which REs are about to expire. You can initiate this query directly from Reason itself.

1. Go under the Reason menu, and you'll notice an option for My Account (see Figure 9.16). Select this.

Figure 9.16 My Account, as seen under the Reason menu.
Source: Propellerhead Software.

2. Once you select My Account, you'll be taken directly to your Account, specifically, your Product page on the Propellerhead website. In this page, select the Rack Extensions tab (see Figure 9.17).

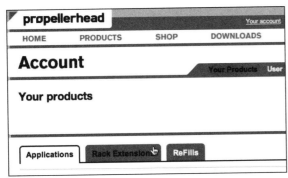

Figure 9.17 My Account page, where I'm about to select the Rack Extensions tab.
Source: Propellerhead Software.

3. On the Rack Extensions page, you get a date for every RE that is about to expire (see Figure 9.18). The REs that are purchased will not have an expiration date.

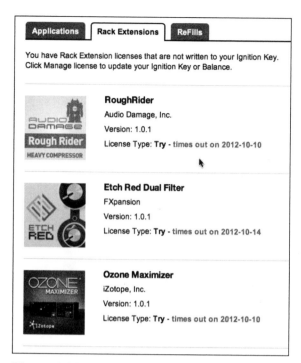

Figure 9.18 All of my Rack Extensions, including the REs that are going to expire soon. Sniff...
Source: Propellerhead Software.

Knowing this little bit of information will keep you ahead of the game when trying REs instead of buying them. If one expires that you can't live without, you can always go back and pick up that missing Rack Extension.

Speaking of trying... Why don't we take a look at some Rack Extensions, individually, now? Let's start with effects.

Rack Extensions: Effects

Some big names in the virtual instrument community have already jumped on board to create some very impressive effects for Reason. Some names you'll recognize, like Izotope, but others are a little newer. But because Propellerhead is keeping a watchful eye on their baby, Reason, all the effects are solid. Since we're talking about Propellerhead, at the moment, let's take a look at what they are offering.

Polar by Propellerhead

Do you ever have need of one of the old vintage harmonizers or pitch shifters? Well, Propellerhead assumed that some people did. After all, these devices have been used and abused in so many ways, to achieve so many different effects from the 1980s on up.

But to just call Polar a pitch-shifter/harmonizer is kind of like calling Reason a music application (see Figure 9.19). It really does far more than just that. You can use Polar as:

▷ A chorus
▷ A delay
▷ A loop device
▷ A stereo fattening device
▷ A MIDI controlled pitch device
▷ A glitch effect device
▷ A harmonizer
▷ A pitch shifter

Yes, the rabbit hole is pretty deep with this one.

Figure 9.19 Polar—the free, pitch-shifting loop device from your good buddies, Propellerhead.
Source: Propellerhead Software.

One thing it's important to do is to go to the Propellerhead product page on the RE shop and watch the videos they've made. They'll give you a very guitar-oriented view of how Polar can be used in the classical sense. And, it's true, Polar can add some depth and beauty to vocals and guitars in ways that will make your head spin. But it's also extremely cool for mangling synthesizer bass lines, drumbeats, drum loops, and just adding straight-up cool, post effects to your songs.

With this in mind, I thought it would be nice to do a little exercise with Polar, where it beats the heck out of Redrum.

Go ahead and "Try" Polar from the Propellerhead website and let's check it out.

Redrum and Polar Together—An Exercise

1. Create a Redrum Drum Computer in a new, empty Reason session, along with a Pulverizer and a Polar. See Figure 9.20.

Figure 9.20 Redrum running through the Pulverizer and Polar.
Source: Propellerhead Software.

2. Set your host tempo to 80 BPM, as shown in Figure 9.21.

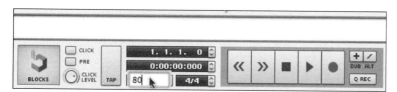

Figure 9.21 The tempo of Reason set to 80 BPM.
Source: Propellerhead Software.

3. Set the Drum Patch of Redrum to Dublab HeavyKit7. This can be found in the Redrum Drum Kits → Heavy Kits folder. See Figure 9.22.

Figure 9.22 Redrum loaded with the Dublab HeavyKit7.
Source: Propellerhead Software.

4. Select the Drum 1 Channel on the Redrum Drum computer. While this drum is selected, click notes 1 and 2, as shown in Figure 9.23. Feel free to have Redrum playing while you program, as I think it makes things more fun.

Figure 9.23 Two kick hits from Redrum on Drum Channel 1.
Source: Propellerhead Software.

5. With Drum Channel 3 selected, select notes 5 and 13 on the Redrum sequencer, as shown in Figure 9.24.

Figure 9.24 The classic snare sequence for Redrum—hits on the 5 and 13.
Source: Propellerhead Software.

6. Select Drum Channel 8 and then press notes 3, 11, 14, and 16 on the Redrum Drum Sequencer, as shown in Figure 9.25.

Figure 9.25 Program a closed hi-hat in the Redrum Drum computer.
Source: Propellerhead Software.

7. On the Pulveriser, bring your Squash up to 1 o'clock, and the Dirt to 3 o'clock, or 81%. See Figure 9.26 for reference.

Figure 9.26 Set up the Pulveriser Squash and Dirt settings.
Source: Propellerhead Software.

8. Now for the fun, Polar-y part! Set your Polar Algorithm to Loop. This setting works much better for drum loops, synth loops, and so on. Then adjust the Delay Buffer to 400 ms (see Figure 9.27).

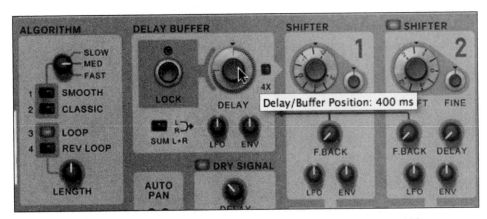

Figure 9.27 Set the Polar Algorithm to Loop and the Delay Buffer to 400 ms.
Source: Propellerhead Software.

9. So far, you're hearing only the delayed signal coming through Polar. This can be wonderful sometimes when you really want to mangle something. But, for our purposes, let's enable the Dry Signal on Polar by pressing the little, red button next to where it says Dry Signal and set the Delay to 11 o'clock or 86 ms (see Figure 9.28). Doing this will allow you to hear the original source from the drums, mostly unaltered, with the exception of a slight delay being contributed by Polar.

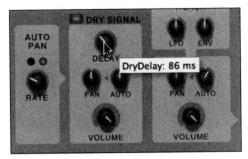

Figure 9.28 Programming Polar's Dry Signal.
Source: Propellerhead Software.

10. Now, let's have some fun with one of Polar's Shifters. Actually, Shifter 1 is actually already active, but it's just not shifting up or down yet. Let's change this. On Shifter 1, turn the Shift down to −19, as shown in Figure 9.29. Immediately, you'll begin to hear a huge difference in your Redrum drum loop, as a separate version of the already playing drum loop is being played along, 19 semitones lower.

Figure 9.29 Shifting down Shifter 1 to 400 ms.
Source: Propellerhead Software.

11. Let's bring Shifter 2 into play now. Click the red button next to where it says Shifter 2. This will enable Shifter 2, and allow you to add some more chaos. Once Shifter 2 is on, set the Shift knob up 17 semitones, as shown in Figure 9.30.

Figure 9.30 Shifter 2 enabled with the Shift knob set to 17 semitones.
Source: Propellerhead Software.

12. Okay, it's probably sounding pretty noisy on your end, at the moment. Different pitched drums are probably flying all over the place, and some may seem a little out of sync. No problem! Let's go ahead and bring in the Filter now to assuage some of those nasty hits and smooth things out a bit. First, enable the Filter by selecting the familiar red button next to it. Then set the Frequency to 3.07 and the Resonance to 66%, as shown in Figure 9.31. These settings will kill some of the more annoying higher end frequencies, while the resonance will give you a small boost in some of the sweeter areas of the loop.

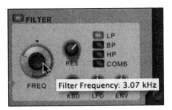

Figure 9.31 The Filter section of Polar.
Source: Propellerhead Software.

13. Now that you have the filter in play, it would be insane not to modulate it, right? Thankfully, Polar has a lovely LFO just waiting to be used. In the LFO section, enable Tempo Sync. The Rate, by default, with Tempo Sync will be set to 2/4, so leave it there. But, in order to hear the LFO in action, you'll need to enable the LFO on the filter. Set the LFO knob in the filter section all the way to the right, at 100%. See Figure 9.32.

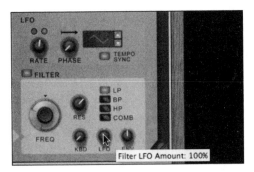

Figure 9.32 The Filter section of Polar.
Source: Propellerhead Software.

Take a listen now. You'll notice that there's a lot going on. The LFO is now sweeping the frequencies we set earlier with the Filter section, and we've got multiple pitched tones going on. And, this was just one, little drumbeat. Polar does some amazing things to your source signal as either a destructive element or an enhancement. You really decide. Oh, and in closing, I should tell you that you can Create Track for Polar as well, from the contextual menu, and use your MIDI controller to play with Polar's pitches. Not bad, right?

Now let's take a look at another wonderful, free Rack Extension for Reason that you really should know about.

Softube Saturation Knob

We don't always need the sledgehammer of distortion that Scream or some of the other distortion devices in Reason offer. Sometimes, we just need incremental, subtle amounts to give basses, vocals, drums, guitars, and so on a little more warmth. Recognizing that Reason was missing a little "subtlety," Softube has made available their amazing Saturation knob as an RE (see Figure 9.33).

Figure 9.33 The Softube Saturation knob.
Source: Softube AB.

The Saturation knob is modeled with output distortion that can be used to add a little body to your bass, presence to your vocals, or just make your drum loops "evil." Because it's one knob and one switch, it doesn't really require much explanation.

Turn the knob, shown in Figure 9.34, to increase the Saturation, or in other words, increase the intensity of the distortion.

Figure 9.34 Turn the Saturation knob.
Source: Softube AB.

The Saturation Type switch gives you a few more options:

▷ Keep High accentuates the high tones, without distorting them. It's good for adding a little shimmer to vocals or bringing out the highs of a lead.
▷ Neutral keeps things at an even playing field in terms of the added frequency of the distortion.
▷ Use the Keep Low setting to preserve low frequencies in sources like bass drums, bass synths, or just to add a little low end to vocals, see Figure 9.35.

Figure 9.35 The Saturation Type switch.
Source: Softube AB.

The Softube Saturation knob really is a device that you'll find yourself using all the time, if you'll just give it a chance. I think a lot of its charm lies in its ease of use with a wonderful, warm sound. And, if you hate it…well, it didn't cost you a dime, anyway. Did it?

Now, what about an effect that can rock your vocals and any other audio you run through it?

Bitspeek by Sonic Charge

I've never really considered myself a groupie for anyone or any band. But, if I had to choose an entity to be a groupie for, it would be Sonic Charge. Outside of Reason, Sonic Charge has been responsible for groundbreaking instruments like MicroTonic and SynPlant. Within Reason, their legacy goes even farther. Magnus Lidstrom, co-founder of Sonic Charge, was actually behind a fair bit of coding within Reason over the last several years. As a matter of fact, Malstrom, within Reason, is one of his babies.

Beyond history, what is Bitspeek (see Figure 9.36)?

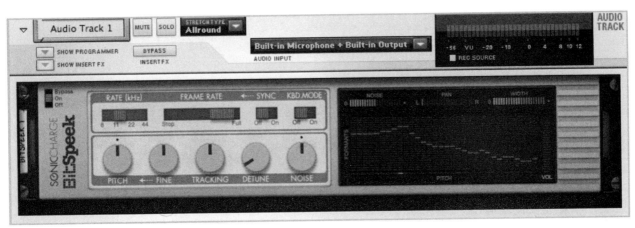

Figure 9.36 Bitspeek, the amazing vocoder from the 1980s, made in the 2000s.
Source: Sonic Charge.
Source: Propellerhead Software.

Remember the old Speak 'n Spells that people have been mangling for years and years for Techno music? Well, so did Sonic Charge! Using the same voice encoding algorithm that the Speak n' Spell used back in the day, Sonic Charge created a form of vocoding that runs your audio through the same algorithm.

The interesting part about Bitspeek, beyond vocoding, is the fact that it will process your vocals without any kind of carrier wave. In fact, it's a device that will give you some wonderful initial gratification, unlike the famous Reason BV512. A device that is so close to a real vocoder that it takes a few minutes to set up...just like a real vocoder.

Another really invaluable function of Bitspeek is its Frame Rate slider. This slider will allow you to lower the buffer speed of the incoming audio in real time. This can create some very interesting "hold" effects and could be really cool for glitching audio, drums, loops, and so on.

So let's get to some instant gratification, if you would like. Just make sure that you download Bitspeek first.

1. In a new Reason session, create an audio track and record some vocals. Make sure you have at least eight measures of audio loop locaters in front and in back of the audio file. This will give you plenty of audio to play with. Also, make sure that you place Reason in Loop mode. See Figure 9.37.

Figure 9.37 An audio track recorded in Reason with the loop points set and loop on.
Source: Propellerhead Software.

2. In the Reason rack, create a Bitspeek device as an insert for your audio track with the vocals (see Figure 9.38).

Figure 9.38 Bitspeek, set up as an insert for an audio track.
Source: Propellerhead Software.
Source: Sonic Charge.

3. Now that we have all the elements in place—those being the audio track and Bitspeek as an insert—let's start playing with Bitspeek. You'll notice, right off the bat, that Bitspeek is doing something very different to your voice. It already sounds much more computer-like, more electronic. This is that famous algorithm that I was referring to earlier, that traces back to the Speak n' Spell. If you recorded dialogue, you'll notice it more than singing. Either way, though, your audio does sound like a robot buddy. If you try adjusting the Rate slider, shown in Figure 9.39, from its default of 22Khz, down to 11, or 8Khz, you'll hear a voice that is even that much more robotic. Give it a try!

Figure 9.39 Adjusting the rate on Bitspeek.
Source: Sonic Charge.

4. I'd also suggest pulling back on the Frame Rate slider. If you pull back on the slider while the audio is playing, you'll notice that Bitspeek will start to slow down your audio, even though it's still playing at the same speed, in the background (see Figure 9.40). This can be cool for transition-type effects in songs, glitches with drums, and so many other fun types of effects.

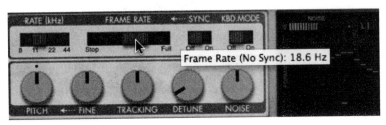

Figure 9.40 Adjusting the Bitspeek Frame Rate slider.
Source: Sonic Charge.

5. This is all well and good, but what about using Bitspeek as a MIDI controlled vocoder? Let's try it out. First, turn KBD Mode: On, on Bitspeek. This will cause your robot to go silent, but have patience! Next, right-click on Bitspeek and select Create Track for Bitspeek 1 (see Figure 9.41).

Figure 9.41 Bitspeek KBD Mode: On, and Reason's Contextual menu.
Source: Sonic Charge.
Source: Propellerhead Software.

6. Now, try playing your MIDI controller while the audio is looping. You'll notice that your keys are controlling your audio's pitch, through Bitspeek. If you want to get that really nasty, thick vocoder sound, try turning the Detune knob up to about 9 o'clock (see Figure 9.42). You'll notice that when you increase the Detune knob amount, the sound gets much thicker. I've found Detune to be especially helpful in getting that thick, nasty robot voice that you hear in some of the older Disco tracks and Sci-Fi shows.

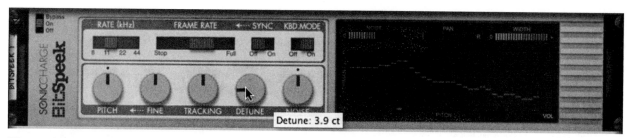

Figure 9.42 Adjusting Bitspeek's Detune.
Source: Sonic Charge.

As you can see, there's a lot of potential for fun and effect with Bitspeek. And you'll be happy to know that there's a lot of fun to be had with the back of Bitspeek as well. With Control Voltage outputs like Pitch, Note, Gate, etc., you can really do some interesting things, like controlling the pitch of synthesizers with your voice and so on.

Now, since we've already taken a bit of a turn into the MIDI controlled effects section of the Rack Extensions store, why don't we go even farther. This next effect is MIDI controlled and so much fun.

Buffre by Peff

If you've ever spent any time online, looking up Reason tutorials, you've probably come across the name "Peff" somewhere along the way. This is the longtime moniker for Reason guru, Kurt Kurasaki. When Rack Extensions became a reality, Kurt was among the first of the Reason fan base to try his hand, along with Hayden Bursk, at creating their own Reason device.

The verdict? Well done, my friends!

Buffre simulates a digital sample buffre that can be triggered at will to create glitches, stutters, stammers, and granular effects out of any audio that you put through it (see Figure 9.43). And, like Polar, it's capable of doing some amazing, almost on-the-fly reverse effects on your audio as well. However, what is really so exciting about Buffre is that it's the first attempt at a an effect like Stutter Edit from Izotope, or Beat Repeat from Ableton Live, right here within Reason.

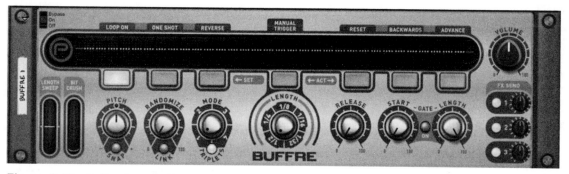

Figure 9.43 Buffre from Peff.
Source: Peff.

But don't let me make you believe that Buffre is any form of a knock-off, just for the Reason community. It's not, at all! In fact, Buffre really is kind of its own thing, in the sense that you can also, to some degree, control the pitch of any incoming audio with your MIDI keyboard.

If you don't own it, try it on the Propellerhead RE shop and give it a whirl.

1. The best way to experience Buffre, in my opinion, is with some drumbeats. I would suggest creating a Dr. Octo Rex in a new Reason session and loading it up with a patch like Elec Drums | Dubstep Loops 140-1.drex in the Reason Factory Soundbank → Dr. Octo Rex → Drums → Electronic Drums → Dubstep folder (see Figure 9.44).

Figure 9.44 Dr. Octo Rex loaded up with a patch.
Source: Propellerhead Software.

2. Next, create a Buffre directly underneath your Dr. Octo Rex. I would also recommend switching your host tempo to 140 BPM as well (see Figure 9.45). Might as well match the tempo of the Dr. Octo Rex loop, right?

Figure 9.45 Dr. Octo Rex running through Buffre while changing the host tempo.
Source: Peff.
Source: Propellerhead Software.

3. Press the spacebar to start Reason's sequencer. You will start Dr. Octo Rex and its endless drumming, which will be graphically displayed in Buffre (see Figure 9.46). While this is taking place, try playing a key on your MIDI controller somewhere within the keys D-1 to D-2. For best results, hold down the key to really hear what's taking place.

Figure 9.46 Dr. Octo Rex beats are displayed in Buffre.
Source: Peff.

Buffre and MIDI Tracks

In most cases, Buffre will automatically make a sequencer track for itself inside of Reason. The only time that it will not do this is if it was created as an insert within the Mix track or an audio track. So, if you want it to create a MIDI track by default, make sure that you create Buffre outside of the Mix and Audio track devices.

4. At this point, you should be having great fun with Buffre and its stutters, glitches, beeps, and so on. Like Bit-speek, which we spoke about in the last section, it's got a lot of instant gratification. Here's a little trick while you're playing around. While holding down a key between D-1 to B-1, try holding down another key in the octave immediately after the first octave. For example, hold down D-0, while holding down D-1, as shown in Figure 9.47. You'll discover that the 0 octave causes sustained notes in the octaves up to pitch up and down.

Figure 9.47 Sustaining keys D-0 and D-1 in on-screen Piano keys.
Source: Propellerhead Software.

As you can see, Buffre can be very addictive to play around with, and it is an awesome effect for any kind of music out there. I would recommend using it sparingly, however. Stutters, and so on, when used excessively can be a little strenuous on the ears. However, there are some people out there that really can make these devices do music in ways never before imagined. Either way, have fun.

Now that we've spent some time with the effects that are out there, I'm going to show you an amazing instrument that you can pick up in the RE format, as well.

RE Instruments

Currently, there aren't a ton of instruments out there for Rack Extensions. Though, as you can imagine, this will change very quickly. At the moment, there are about two to three instruments, and all of them are great. However, I'd like to talk to you about the absolute "must have" synth that is currently available.

Korg Polysix

To have an old and reputable name like Korg being added to the lineup of synthesizers within Reason is quite simply incredible (see Figure 9.48). After all, Korg has brought us some of the most classic synthesizers in synthesizer history —for example: the MS-20, the Poly-800, the Wavestation, and, of course, the Polysix.

Figure 9.48 The Korg Polysix as it appears in Reason.
Source: Korg.

A few years back, Korg began introducing software versions of their classic synths in the form of their own Legacy line of VST, AU, and RTAS plug-ins. Unlike others in the past who have simply slapped in some oscillators, envelopes, and LFOs into some software and named it after a classic synthesizer, Korg went a lot farther. Developing CMT, or Component Modeling Technology, the Korg Legacy line more than vaguely resembled the classic instruments; they actually sounded just like them. Or as close as you could get in software.

When Korg announced that they would be joining the growing list of RE makers for Reason, many wondered if the same quality of work that they had done in the past would carry over.

Yep, it did.

The Polysix boasts all of the features that it is known for in the Legacy Series of plug-ins. As a matter of fact, the Polysix even includes all the U.S. expansion patches included in with the original! And, to make things even better, it also has two assignable CV inputs on the back that, through the front panel, can be used to modulate functions within the Polysix like:

▷ VCO Pulse Width
▷ VCF Cutoff
▷ VCA Gain
▷ MG Level

Let's have a little CV fun with the Polysix right now. Make sure that you've "tried" it from the RE shop and restarted.

1. In a new Reason session, create a Korg Polysix and Matrix Pattern Sequencer. Since we're playing around with Control Voltages, why don't we go with an old CV favorite? See Figure 9.49.

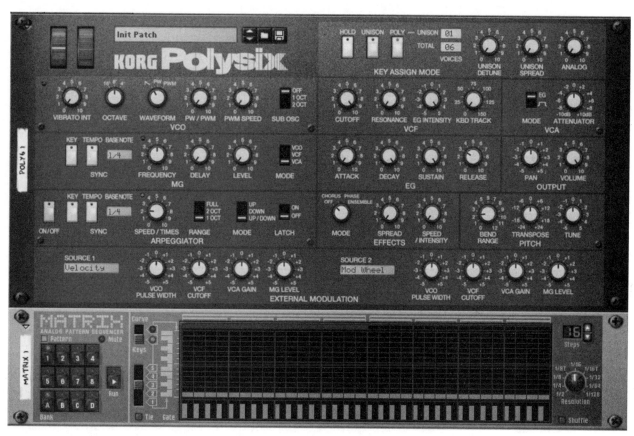

Figure 9.49 The Korg Polysix with a Matrix Pattern Sequencer.
Source: Korg.
Source: Propellerhead Software.

2. Set Reason's host tempo to 80 BPM. This will give you a slower tempo to groove in. Once the tempo is set, program a Matrix pattern that you don't mind listening to for a bit. (No picture shown.)

3. Press the Tab button and drag a cable from the Curve out of the Matrix to CV 1 on the Polysix (see Figure 9.50). This will allow the Curve signal sent from the Matrix to modulate the available parameters in the External Modulation section of the Polysix. But, before this will really happen, you'll need to set it up within the Polysix.

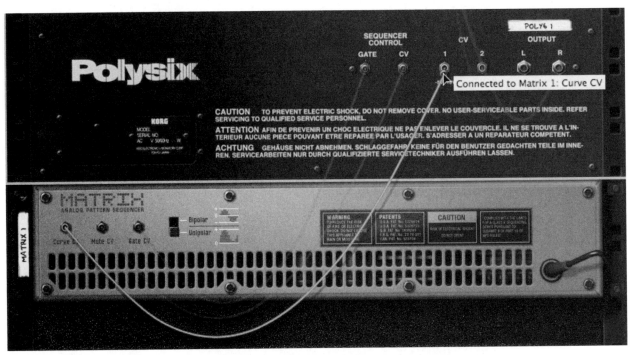

Figure 9.50 Curve Control Voltage going to the Polysix.
Source: Korg.
Source: Propellerhead Software.

4. Back on the front of the Polysix, set Source 1, via the Source 1 drop-down menu to CV1 (see Figure 9.51). This will tell the Polysix to use the incoming Curve signal of the Matrix as the modulation source.

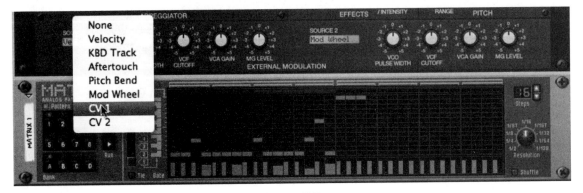

Figure 9.51 Switching the Source 1 modulation to CV1.
Source: Korg.
Source: Propellerhead Software.

5. In the Source 1 subsection of the External Modulation section of the Polysix, increase the VCF Cutoff all the way to the right. This will give the Curve of the Matrix a lot of the power of the filter within Polysix. Set the Matrix to Curve mode and draw in a slope for your sequence (see Figure 9.52).

Figure 9.52 The External Modulation section of the Polysix and the Matrix in Curve mode.
Source: Korg.
Source: Propellerhead Software.

6. If you're listening so far, you'll realize that nothing is happening. Well, this will change after this step, if you've been following along. The first thing is to turn down the EG Intensity, which diminishes the power of the envelope in which it is tied to. By turning it to about +2, this will greatly help our cause. But, to make things, finally, audible, also turn the Cutoff in the VCF section all the way down. And, if you want to make things really interesting, turn the Resonance up to about 5 (see Figure 9.53).

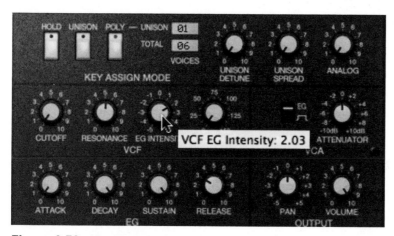

Figure 9.53 The External Modulation section of the Polysix and the Matrix in Curve mode.
Source: Korg.

Keep in mind, the Polysix has two CV inputs, and they both are brought into action within the External Modulation section of the Polysix. The second CV input can be used simultaneously with the first by setting Source 2 in the External Modulation section to CV2.

This small exercise only gave you a taste of what's possible with the Polysix. In getting to know it, I would highly encourage you to check out the plethora of patches that Korg supplied with its release. The patches are all quite usable, but in the event that they don't tickle your fancy, well, it's an extremely fun synth to program as well!

Conclusion

If this section and the tasty REs that were spotlighted herein didn't start you salivating, then I would suggest getting in the Propellerhead Shop for REs and finding some that work for you. Really, there are more and more being added each day, and as I mentioned before, there are no slouches jumping into the development of REs. There are a lot of talented people and companies getting involved. Besides, you can try them all out for a few weeks anyway. What do you have to lose?

Index

A

adding
  effects (effects Combinators), 148–151
  lanes (tracks), 83
  MIDI controllers, 7–9
Alligator
  control voltages, 184–185
  inserts, 185–188
  overview, 183–184
applications, Reason comparison, 14
arrows, remixing blocks, 52
AU (Rack Extensions), 192
audio. *See also* **MIDI**
  Audio Tracks (Combinators), 146
  bouncing Rack Extension tracks, 198–201
  buffer size, 3
  built-in, 2
  converting to samples (Kong), 108–116
  disabling, 30
  input, 2
  pitch (Kong), 116
  preferences, 1–3, 97
  Sampling Input, 3–6
  velocity (Kong), 116
Audio Tracks (Combinators), 146
auto quantizing (Q Rec) 23
Auto-Tune. *See* **Neptune**

B

back panel
  BV512 Vocoder, 176–177
  Rack Extensions, 192–193
background vocals (Neptune), 174
beats (Redrum drums)
  drawing, 54–55
  playing, 55
Bitspeek, 212–214
Block mode, 39–41

blocks. *See also* **loops**
  as a marker system, 37–42
  Block mode, 39–41
  choruses, 41
  colors, 39, 42
  drawing, 39–40
  enabling, 38
  overview, 37
  remixing
    arrows, 52
    copying, 46
    creating blocks, 43–44
    cutting, 45
    deleting, 50
    dragging, 45
    drawing, 51
    handlebars, 52
    loop points, 47
    pasting, 46–47
    pitch, 52
    selecting all, 49
    size, 52
    smoothing, 48
    Snap resolution, 43
    tap tempo, 52
    tempo, 52
    tightening, 43–44
  text, 39–41
  verses, 39–41
bouncing Rack Extension tracks to audio, 198–201
breaks (Redrum drums), 58–59
Browse Patch (effects Combinators), 147–148
buffer size (audio), 3
Buffre, 215–217
built-in audio, 2
built-in input, 2
built-in microphones, 2
built-in output, 2
buttons, RV7000 Advanced Reverb mapping, 155–158

BV512 Vocoder
  back panel, 176–177
  control voltages, 176–177
  overview, 175–176
  Robotic effects, 177–182
bypassing effects (effects Combinators), 151–152

C

channels
  layout, 85
  Mix Channels. *See* Mix Channels
  selecting (Redrum drums), 54–55
choruses (blocks), 41
click tracks, 24
colors
  blocks, 39, 42
  Mix Channels (drums), 76
Combinators
  Audio Tracks, 146
  effects Combinators. *See* effects Combinators
  inputs, 146
  Mix Channel comparison, 76
  Mix Channels, 146
  outputs, 146
  overview, 121–122
  Subtractor and Matrix
    control voltages, 125–127, 136, 138–140
    creating, 122–133
    curves, 127–128, 130
    Echo effect, 133–138
    effects, 133–143
    gates, 125–128
    key mapping, 142–143
    LFOs, 134, 136–137, 141
    oscillators, 140–141
    patterns, 128–132
    phaser effect, 138–142
    pitch, 135, 137–138
    Pulveriser effect, 138–142

Index

Combinators (*Continued*)
    randomizing, 129–130
    thickening, 141
    Tie button, 128
    velocity, 128
commands (keyboard commands)
    mixer, 17
    overview, 14
    piano keyboard, 19
    rack, 16
    sequencer, 15
    Tool window, 18
condensing (Mix Channels), 91
control voltages (CVs), 121
    Alligator, 184–185
    BV512 Vocoder, 176–177
    Combinators (Subtractor and Matrix),
        125–127, 136, 138–140
    Neptune, 168–169
    overview, 121–122
    Rack Extensions, 192–193
controllers
    mapping (Kong), 105
    setup
        adding MIDI controllers, 7–9
        finding, 6–7
        multiple MIDI controllers, 9–10
        overview, 6–7
        Rewire, 10
converting
    audio to samples (Kong), 108–116
    patterns to MIDI, 61–63
copying
    MIDI notes, 32–33
    patterns, 55
    remixing blocks, 46
Count-in, 24–25
creating
    blocks
        drawing, 39–40, 51
        remixing, 43–44, 51
    Combinators (Subtractor and Matrix),
        122–133
    default songs, 11
    drawing
        blocks, 39–40
        MIDI notes, 33
        patterns, 58–59
        Redrum beats, 54–55
        Redrum breaks, 58–59
        remixing blocks, 51
    drums (Redrum)
        beats, 54–55
        breaks, 58–59
        drum machines, 53
        hi-hats, 56–57
        Mix Channels, 67–76
        outputs, 67–76

    pattern lanes, 57–58
    snare rolls, 57
    snares, 55
    tracks, 63–67
    instruments, 19–23
    Mix Channels
        devices, 124
        drums, 67–76
        effects Combinators, 161–165
curves (Combinators), 127–128, 130
**Cut EQ (Scream Sound Destruction),
    154–155**
cutting (remixing blocks), 45
CVs (control voltages), 121
    Alligator, 184–185
    BV512 Vocoder, 176–177
    Combinators (Subtractor and Matrix),
        125–127, 136, 138–140
    Neptune, 168–169
    overview, 121–122
    Rack Extensions, 192–193
cymbals, 82–87

D

**dates, trial Rack Extension expiration,
    201–203**
default songs, 10–11
deleting (remixing blocks), 50
disabling
    audio, 30
    effects, 151–152
distortion (Scream Sound Destruction)
    Cut EQ, 154–155
    effects Combinators, 148–155
    filtering, 154–155
    parameter knobs, 152–154
    rotary knobs, 152–154
Dr. Octo Rex
    effects Combinators. *See* effects
        Combinators
    sampling, 97
dragging
    MIDI notes, 31
    remixing blocks, 45
drawing. *See also* **creating**
    blocks, 39–40
    MIDI notes, 33
    patterns, 58–59
    Redrum drums
        beats, 54–55
        breaks, 58–59
    remixing blocks, 51
drums
    Buffre, 215–217
    creating colors, 76
    creating Mix Channels, 67–76
    creating outputs, 67–76

    cymbals, 82–87
    dub tracks, 82–87
    fills, 82–87
    grouping, 67, 76
    insert effects, 76–82
    mapping, 3–4
    MIDI
        converting patterns to MIDI, 61–63
        splitting into separate tracks, 63–67
    Mix Channels, colors, 76
    Rack Extensions, 205–210
    remixing
        copying patterns, 55
        creating hi-hats, 56–57
        creating pattern lanes, 57–58
        creating Redrum drum machines, 53
        creating snare rolls, 57
        creating snares, 55
        drawing beats, 54–55
        drawing breaks, 58–59
        drawing patterns, 58–59
        loading, 54
        overview, 53
        pasting patterns, 55
        playing beats, 55
        selecting channels, 54–55
        tempo, 56
        velocity, 57
    reverb, 76–82
    rotary knobs, 76–82
    sampling, 97–101
    sidechaining, 87–93
    tracks
        grouping, 67, 76
        splitting, 63–67
dub tracks (drums), 82–87

E

Echo effect (Combinators), 133–138
editing MIDI
    copying notes, 32–33
    disabling sound, 30
    dragging notes, 31
    drawing notes, 33
    note length, 31–32
    note velocity, 34
    overview, 29
    playing notes, 30
    viewing note information, 31
effects (FX), 76
    adding (effects Combinators), 148–151
    Alligator
        control voltages, 184–185
        inserts, 185–188
        overview, 183–184
    BV512 Vocoder
        back panel, 176–177

control voltages, 176–177
overview, 175–176
Robotic effects, 177–182
bypassing (effects Combinators),
151–152
Combinators (Subtractor and Matrix),
133–143
disabling (effects Combinators),
151–152
Echo, 133–138
effects Combinators. *See* effects
Combinators
insert effects (drums), 76–82
MIDI controlled effects
overview, 167
setup, 171–173
Neptune
background vocals, 174
control voltages, 168–169
inserts, 169
overview, 167–168
Robotic effects, 169–171
setup, 171–173
patching order (effects Combinators),
149
phaser, 138–142
Pulveriser, 138–142
Rack Extensions
Bitspeek, 212–214
Buffre, 215–217
Polar, 203–210
Redrum, 205–210
Saturation knob, 210–211
reverb (drums), 76–82
effects Combinators
Browse Patch, 147–148
creating Mix Channels, 161–165
effects
adding, 148–151
bypassing, 151–152
disabling, 151–152
patching order, 149
loops, loading, 147–148
overview, 145–146
refills, 160–161
RV7000 Advanced Reverb, 148–152,
155–160
EQ, 159
mapping buttons, 155–158
Room Algorithm, 157–158
rotary knobs, 156–158
tap, 155–158
Tempo Sync, 157
saving, 160
Scream Sound Destruction,
148–155
Cut EQ, 154–155
filtering, 154–155

parameter knobs, 152–154
rotary knobs, 152–154
embedding samples in files, 114
enabling blocks, 38
EQ (RV7000 Advanced Reverb), 159
**expiration (trial Rack Extensions),
198–203**
extensions. *See* **Rack Extensions**

F

files, embedding samples, 114
fills (drums), 82–87
filters
Alligator gates
control voltages, 184–185
inserts, 185–188
overview, 183–184
Scream Sound Destruction, 154–155
finding MIDI controllers, 6–7
folders (Scratch Disk folder), 11–12
FX. *See* **effects**

G

gates
Alligator
control voltages, 184–185
inserts, 185–188
overview, 183–184
Combinators (Subtractor and Matrix),
125–128
grand piano (NN-XT), 116–119
grouping drum tracks, 67, 76

H

handlebars (remixing blocks), 52
hard drives, space, 11
hi-hats (Redrum drums), 56–57
hits, mapping multiple, 106–108

I

inputs
Combinators, 146
sampling
mapping, 96–97
setup, 3–6
inserts
Alligator, 185–188
drums, 76–82
Neptune, 169
installing Rack Extensions, 193–197
instruments
creating, 19–23
MIDI recording, 25–29
Rack Extensions (Korg Polysix),
218–221

sampling
Kong. *See* Kong
NN-19, overview, 96
NN-Nano. *See* Kong
NN-XT, 116–119
overview, 95–96
Redrum. *See* Redrum
setup
click tracks, 24
Loop mode, 23–24
Pre (Count-in), 24–25
Q Rec (Auto Quantize), 23
tap tempo, 25
tempo, 25
time signature, 25

K

key mapping (Combinators), 142–143
keyboards
commands
mixer, 17
overview, 14
piano keyboard, 19
rack, 16
sequencer, 15
Tool window, 18
MIDI. *See* MIDI
NN-XT, 116–119
Kong
mapping
multiple hits, 106–108
MIDI controllers, 105
velocity mapping, 101–106
pitch, 105–106
sampling
converting audio, 108–116
embedding in files, 114
pitch, 116
velocity, 116
Korg Polysix, 218–221

L

lanes (tracks), 83
layout (channels), 85
length (MIDI notes), 31–32
**LFOs (low frequency oscillators), 134,
136–137, 141**
libraries (effects Combinators), 160–161
loading
loops (effects Combinators), 147–148
Redrum drums, 54
Loop mode, instrument setup, 23–24
loop points, remixing blocks, 47
loops
blocks. *See* blocks
loading (effects Combinators), 147–148

Index

loops (*Continued*)
Loop mode, 23–24
loop points, remixing blocks, 47
**low frequency oscillators (LFOs), 134,
136–137, 141**

M
mapping
drums, 3–4
key mapping (Combinators), 142–143
Kong
MIDI controllers, 105
multiple hits, 106–108
velocity mapping, 101–106
NN-XT, 116–119
RV7000 Advanced Reverb buttons,
155–158
sampling inputs, 3–6, 96–97
marker system (blocks), 37–42
Matrix and Subtractor Combinator
control voltages, 125–127, 136, 138–140
creating, 122–133
curves, 127–128, 130
Echo effect, 133–138
effects, 133–143
gates, 125–128
key mapping, 142–143
LFOs, 134, 136–137, 141
oscillators, 140–141
patterns, 128–132
phaser effect, 138–142
pitch, 135, 137–138
Pulveriser effect, 138–142
randomizing, 129–130
thickening, 141
Tie button, 128
velocity, 128
metronome (click tracks), 24
microphones, built-in, 2
MIDI. *See also* **audio**
Alligator
control voltages, 184–185
inserts, 185–188
overview, 183–184
BV512 Vocoder
back panel, 176–177
control voltages, 176–177
overview, 175–176
Robotic effects, 177–182
drums, converting patterns, 61–63
editing
copying notes, 32–33
disabling sound, 30
dragging notes, 31
drawing notes, 33
note length, 31–32
note velocity, 34

overview, 29
playing notes, 30
viewing note information, 31
MIDI controlled effects
overview, 167
setup, 171–173
MIDI controllers
adding MIDI controllers, 7–9
finding, 6–7
mapping (Kong), 105
multiple MIDI controllers, 9–10
overview, 6–7
Rewire, 10
Neptune
background vocals, 174
control voltages, 168–169
inserts, 169
overview, 167–168
Robotic effects, 169–171
setup, 171–173
recording, 25–29
MIDI controlled effects
overview, 167
setup, 171–173
MIDI controllers
mapping (Kong), 105
setup
adding MIDI controllers, 7–9
finding, 6–7
multiple MIDI controllers, 9–10
overview, 6–7
Rewire, 10
Mix Channels
Combinators, 146
comparison, 76
creating effects Combinators,
161–165
condensing, 91
drums
colors, 76
creating, 67–76
racks, 124
mixer, opening, 17
mixing. *See* **remixing**
moving (dragging)
MIDI notes, 31
remixing blocks, 45
**Multi Tap (RV7000 Advanced Reverb),
155–158**
multiple hits (Kong), 106–108
multiple MIDI controllers, 9–10

N
navigation (keyboard commands)
mixer, 17
overview, 14
piano keyboard, 19

rack, 16
sequencer, 15
Tool window, 18
Neptune
background vocals, 174
control voltages, 168–169
inserts, 169
overview, 167–168
Robotic effects, 169–171
setup, 171–173
NN-19, overview, 96
NN-Nano. *See* **Kong**
NN-XT, 116–119
notes (MIDI)
copying, 32–33
dragging, 31
drawing, 33
length, 31–32
playing, 30
velocity, 34
viewing information, 31

O
opening
mixer, 17
piano keyboard, 19
rack, 16
sequencer, 15
Tool window, 18
order, patching effects, 149
oscillators
Combinators, 140–141
LFOs (low frequency oscillators), 134,
136–137, 141
outputs
built-in, 2
Combinators, 146
drums, 67–76

P
**parameter knobs (Scream Sound
Destruction), 152–154**
pasting
patterns, 55
remixing blocks, 46–47
patching effects, order, 149
pattern lanes (Redrum drums), 57–58
patterns
Combinators, 128–132
converting to MIDI, 61–63
copying, 55
drawing, 58–59
pasting, 55
pattern lanes (Redrum drums), 57–58
Peff Buffre, 215–217
Pencil. *See* **drawing**

phaser effect (Combinators), 138–142
piano
    NN-XT, 116–119
    opening keyboard, 19
pitch
    Combinators, 135–138
    Kong, 105–106, 116
    Neptune
        background vocals, 174
        control voltages, 168–169
        inserts, 169
        overview, 167–168
        Robotic effects, 169–171
        setup, 171–173
    remixing blocks, 52
playing
    MIDI notes, 30
    Redrum beats, 55
plug-ins. See Rack Extensions
Polar, 203–210
Polysix, 218–221
Pre (Count-in), 24–25
preferences. See setup
Propellerhead Polar, 203–210
Pulveriser effect (Combinators),
    138–142

Q–R

Q Rec (Auto Quantize) instrument
    setup, 23
quantizing. See Q Rec (Auto Quantize)
Rack Extensions (REs)
    AU, 192
    back panel, 192, 193
    bouncing tracks to audio, 198–201
    checking expiration dates, 201–203
    control voltages, 192–193
    effects
        Bitspeek, 212–214
        Buffre, 215–217
        Polar, 203–210
        Redrum, 205–210
        Saturation knob, 210–211
    installing, 193–197
    Korg Polysix instrument, 218–221
    overview, 191
    trial expiration, 198–201
    VST, 192
racks
    Mix Channels, 124
    opening, 16
    Rack Extensions. See Rack Extensions
randomizing (Combinators), 129–130
Razor (remixing blocks), 45
Reason, other applications
    comparison, 14
recording (MIDI), 25–29

Redrum, 205–210
    colors, 76
    converting patterns to MIDI, 61–63
    copying patterns, 55
    creating
        hi-hats, 56–57
        Mix Channels, 67–76
        outputs, 67–76
        pattern lanes, 57–58
        Redrum drum machines, 53
        snare rolls, 57
        snares, 55
    cymbals, 82–87
    drawing
        beats, 54–55
        breaks, 58–59
        patterns, 58–59
    dub tracks, 82–87
    fills, 82–87
    grouping, 67, 76
    insert effects, 76–82
    loading, 54
    overview, 53
    pasting patterns, 55
    playing beats, 55
    reverb, 76–82
    rotary knobs, 76–82
    sampling, 97–101
    selecting channels, 54–55
    sidechaining, 87–93
    splitting into separate tracks, 63–67
    tempo, 56
    velocity, 57
refills (effects Combinators), 160–161
remixing
    blocks
        arrows, 52
        copying, 46
        creating blocks, 43–44
        cutting, 45
        deleting, 50
        dragging, 45
        drawing, 51
        handlebars, 52
        loop points, 47
        pasting, 46–47
        pitch, 52
        selecting all, 49
        size, 52
        smoothing, 48
        Snap resolution, 43
        tap tempo, 52
        tempo, 52
        tightening, 43–44
    drums
        copying patterns, 55
        creating hi-hats, 56–57
        creating pattern lanes, 57–58

        creating Redrum drum machines, 53
        creating snare rolls, 57
        creating snares, 55
        drawing beats, 54–55
        drawing breaks, 58–59
        drawing patterns, 58–59
        loading, 54
        overview, 53
        pasting patterns, 55
        playing beats, 55
        selecting channels, 54–55
        tempo, 56
        velocity, 57
REs. See Rack Extensions
resolution (remixing blocks), 43
reverb
    drums, 76–82
    RV7000 Advanced Reverb
        effects Combinators, 148–160
        EQ, 159
        mapping buttons, 155–158
        Room Algorithm, 157–158
        rotary knobs, 156–158
        tap, 155–158
        Tempo Sync, 157
Rewire (MIDI controllers), 10
Robotic effects
    Bitspeek, 212–214
    BV512 Vocoder, 177–182
    Neptune, 169–171
Room Algorithm (RV7000 Advanced
    Reverb), 157–158
rotary knobs
    drums, 76–82
    RV7000 Advanced Reverb, 156–158
    Scream Sound Destruction, 152–154
RV7000 Advanced Reverb, 148–152,
    155–160
    EQ, 159
    mapping buttons, 155–158
    Room Algorithm, 157–158
    rotary knobs, 156–158
    tap, 155–158
    Tempo Sync, 157

S

sampling
    Dr. Octo Rex, 97
    embedding in files, 114
    input
        mapping, 96–97
        setup, 3–6
    instruments
        Kong. See Kong
        NN-19, overview, 96
        NN-Nano. See Kong
        NN-XT, 116–119

Index

sampling (*Continued*)
> overview, 95–96
> Redrum. *See* Redrum
> overview, 95

Saturation knob, 210–211
saving (effects Combinators), 160
Scratch Disk folder, 11–12
Scream Sound Destruction, 148–155
> Cut EQ, 154–155
> filtering, 154–155
> parameter knobs, 152–154
> rotary knobs, 152–154

selecting
> channels (Redrum drums), 54–55
> selecting all (remixing blocks), 49

sequencer
> opening, 15
> other applications comparison, 14

setup
> audio preferences, 1–3, 97
> default songs, 10–11
> drums, 3–4
> instruments
>> click tracks, 24
>> Loop mode, 23–24
>> Pre (Count-in), 24–25
>> Q Rec (Auto Quantize), 23
>> tap tempo, 25
>> tempo, 25
>> time signature, 25
> MIDI controlled effects, 171–173
> MIDI controllers
>> adding MIDI controllers, 7–9
>> finding, 6–7
>> multiple MIDI controllers, 9–10
>> overview, 6–7
>> Rewire, 10
> Neptune, 171–173
> Sampling Input, 3–6
> Scratch Disk folder, 11–12
> Setup Wizard, 1

Setup Wizard, 1
sidechaining (drums), 87–93
singing. *See* vocals
size
> buffer size, 3
> remixing blocks, 52

smoothing (remixing blocks), 48
Snap resolution (remixing blocks), 43
snare rolls (Redrum drums), 57
snares (Redrum drums), 55

Softube Saturation knob, 210–211
songs (default songs), 10–11
Sonic Charge, Bitspeek, 212–214
sound. *See* audio
space (hard drives), 11
special effects. *See* effects
splitting drums, 63–67
Subtractor and Matrix Combinator
> control voltages, 125–127, 136, 138–140
> creating, 122–133
> curves, 127–128, 130
> Echo effect, 133–138
> effects, 133–143
> gates, 125–128
> key mapping, 142–143
> LFOs, 134, 136–137, 141
> oscillators, 140–141
> patterns, 128–132
> phaser effect, 138–142
> pitch, 135, 137–138
> Pulveriser effect, 138–142
> randomizing, 129–130
> thickening, 141
> Tie button, 128
> velocity, 128

T

tap (RV7000 Advanced Reverb), 155–158
tap tempo
> instrument setup, 25
> remixing blocks, 52

templates (default songs), 10–11
tempo
> instrument setup, 25
> Redrum drums, 56
> remixing blocks, 52
> Tempo Sync (RV7000 Advanced Reverb), 157

Tempo Sync (RV7000 Advanced Reverb), 157
text (blocks), 39–41
thickening (Combinators), 141
third-party tools. *See* Rack Extensions
Tie button (Combinators), 128
tightening (remixing blocks), 43–44
time signature, instrument setup, 25
Tool window, opening, 18
tracks
> bouncing Rack Extension to audio, 198–201

click tracks, 24
drums
> grouping, 67, 76
> splitting, 63–67
> dub tracks (drums), 82–87
> lanes, adding, 83

trial Rack Extensions
> checking expiration dates, 201–203
> expiration, 198–201

triple-filtered gates (Alligator)
> control voltages, 184–185
> inserts, 185–188
> overview, 183–184

tuning instruments (NN-XT), 116–119

V–W

velocity
> Combinators (Subtractor and Matrix), 128
> MIDI notes, 34
> Redrum drums, 57
> Kong
>> mapping, 101–106
>> sampling, 116

verses (blocks), 39–41
viewing notes information, 31
vocals
> Bitspeek, 212–214
> BV512 Vocoder
>> back panel, 176–177
>> control voltages, 176–177
>> overview, 175–176
>> Robotic effects, 177–182
> Neptune
>> background vocals, 174
>> control voltages, 168–169
>> inserts, 169
>> overview, 167–168
>> Robotic effects, 169–171
>> setup, 171–173

vocoders
> Bitspeek, 212–214
> BV512 Vocoder
>> back panel, 176–177
>> control voltages, 176–177
>> overview, 175–176
>> Robotic effects, 177–182

voltages. *See* control voltages
VST, Rack Extensions, 192
wizard, Setup Wizard, 1